My NESCO

SnackMaster Pro Dehydrator

Recipe Book

100 DELICIOUS EVERY-DAY RECIPES INCLUDING JERKY, TEA, & POTPOURRI!

BY

AMANDA PHILLIPS

Bay City Press

BAY CITY PRESS
SANTA MONICA, CA

Customer Reviews

"*These recipes come with nutrition information and this book offers a wide variety of simple and tasty options. Knowing the amount of calories, fat, carbs, etc. is important to us. We've had a lot of success with this machine*" -Kelly A.

"*This book opened a new world for me. I'm never going back to store-bought chips, spices, snacks, when I can save money and make sure my kids aren't eating junk. This is my favorite appliance by far. It has changed the game in our kitchen*" -Amy C.

"*Provides a lot of super easy and great tasting recipes and information. Someone did their homework here*" – Timothy R.

Easy to follow instructions got us up and running super quickly and we're still learning more fun stuff about dehydrators. Thank you!" - Marketa T.

"*The peach cobbler recipe in this book is amazing. Also, I'm big on snacking throughout the day and I've found that mixing these recipes with nuts has been a very satisfying and fun change in the way I manage my diet. I love fruit rolls and dried fruit etc and this book has not disappointed.*" – Beth K

"*I was worried, but my kids love the fruit rolls. Also, my husband and I tried a couple of the jerky recipes and were pleasantly surprised by how much we loved them.*" -Barbara C

Legal Notice

All content herein represents the author's own experiences and opinions. The information written, illustrated and presented in this book is for the purpose of entertainment only. The author does not assume any liability for the use of or inability to use any or all of the information contained in this book, and does not accept responsibility for any type of loss or damage that may be experienced by the user as the result of activities occurring from the use of any information in this book. Use the information at your own risk. The author reserves the right to make changes he or she deems required to future versions of the publication to maintain accuracy.

ISBN -13: 978-1720481218

ISBN- 10: 1720481210

Published in the United States of America by Bay City Press

Table Of Contents

1

WHY YOU NEED THIS BOOK!

Get Started Right Now with Our Easy Instructions

Congratulations on your purchase of the Nesco SnackMaster Pro Food Dehydrator! If you're new to the world of food dehydrating, you may have a lot of questions about how to get started. Luckily, our easy to follow instructions will have you on your way to delicious dehydrated treats in no time. This guide will provide you with all the information you need to dry meats, fruits, vegetables and so much more. Simply refer to this guide for everything you need to know about using your Nesco SnackMaster like a pro.

Get the Most from Your Nesco SnackMaster with This in Depth, Real World Guide

By now you probably know that you can make your own dried fruits and meat jerky at home, but did you know that you can also make nutritious powders and fragrant tea blends with the Nesco SnackMaster? This in-depth guide will teach you plenty of exciting ways to turn your favorite fruits and meats into healthy and delicious treats, but you'll also learn valuable techniques for how to get the absolute most out of your SnackMaster. From choosing temperature and time settings, to learning how to best arrange food in the dehydrator, we take all of the guess work out of making amazing meals and snacks that will delight the entire family. In addition to easy-to-follow instructions and tips, we will also explore the science and history of food dehydration to give you an understanding of all the benefits of using a dehydrator at home. And did you know dehydrating food is an amazing way to save money? This book will show you ways to get the most out of your ingredients, so you can really see the savings.

Amazing Pro Tips for Making All Kinds of Dehydrated Foods

Once you've learned the basics of dehydration it's time to become a pro. This book will teach you everything you need to know to take your dehydration game to the next level with tips developed to maximize your dehydrating results. Not only can use your dehydrator for purposes other than dehydrating food, but did you know you can change temperature settings to speed up your results? Our pro tips section will teach you tricks you won't find anywhere else, and everything you need to know in order to get the most value from your Nesco SnackMaster.

100 Amazing Recipes You Won't Find Anywhere Else!

Your Nesco SnackMaster is perfect for making dehydrated classics like jerkies and dried fruit, but our exciting and diverse recipes go far beyond traditional snacks, providing you with endless possibilities for amazing breakfasts, entrees, desserts, sides, and even soups and stews! With so many unique recipes not found anywhere else, this guide will be a valuable tool as you navigate the wide world of dehydration. We will even give you step by step instructions on how to make all-natural air fresheners and potpourri, which are not only useful around the house, but contain no artificial chemicals or dyes. This is truly the only guide you will ever need for using the Nesco SnackMaster food dehydrator.

Avoid Common Mistakes and Become a Dehydrating Pro

The Nesco SnackMaster is the easiest food dehydrator on the market today, but if you've never used a food dehydrator before, getting started might seem a little challenging. Luckily, this guide will show you how to avoid common mistakes and put you on a path to be a dehydrator expert in no time. From avoiding food sticking to the trays to figuring out how to master the SnackMaster's settings and controls, we will carefully walk you through the techniques for producing perfect snacks from your very first batch. We will also teach you the best methods for cleaning and storing the SnackMaster to improve your chances of getting perfect results for many years to come.

2

THE WONDERFUL WORLD OF
FOOD DEHYDRATORS

How Do Food Dehydrators Work?

Food dehydration has been around for thousands of years, but the modern food dehydrator does the job more reliably and in a fraction of the time. Dehydrators work by controlling temperature, while creating air flow to remove moisture from your food. The combination of low heat and constant air flow results in uniformly dried food. Because the moisture in food is what helps cause it to spoil, removing most of the moisture means your food lasts far longer than before it was dehydrated. The Nesco SnackMaster works using the unique Fan Flow Radial Air system which results in even dehydration in less time than other commercially available models. It also means you don't have to monitor your food and move it to make sure it comes out evenly. Unlike the canning process the Nesco SnackMaster maintains a low heat, which results in the preservation of valuable nutrients that are lost at higher heat. To give you even more flexibility the Nesco SnackMaster is expandable so you can make even more dehydrated foods at once.

A Brief History of Food Dehydration

Believe it or not, dehydration to preserve food has been around for over 14,000 years. Dating back to 12,000 B.C. in the Middle East and Asia, food dehydration was a technique used by humans before refrigeration came into existence. Those early humans figured out that harmful bacteria and yeasts were responsible for their food going bad, and they realized the culprit: water. They discovered that if they removed most of the water from meat and fruits, they did not spoil quickly and could be safely stored far longer. Originally, the dehydration was accomplished by sun drying food, though this was not a very reliable method for drying many types of food. Eventually, humans figured out that smoking foods produced a more reliable way to dehydrate food, but smoking food isn't very efficient and really only works well for meats. The invention of home food dehydrators changed everything, and people suddenly had the option to easily make dehydrated foods in the comfort of their own home. The Nesco SnackMaster continues this ancient tradition of food dehydration, but with some help from modern science.

Who Uses Food Dehydrators?

If you love delicious dried foods that are cheaper and healthier than store bought dried foods, food dehydration is for you. Store bought meat jerkies are expensive and only come in a small variety of flavors. With your Nesco SnackMaster food dehydrator you get to be in control of what you make. You decide which cuts of meat to dehydrate, and you can custom tailor your seasonings to make your jerky taste exactly how you want. Many people these days are rightfully concerned about the dangers of added sugar in snacks. The great thing about using the Nesco SnackMaster to dehydrate your own foods is you get to control how much sugar is included. Now you can make snacks that are healthier and lower in sugar, so you can enjoy your snacks more. This is perfect for parents who want healthy but tasty snacks for kids. And because using the SnackMaster is safe and easy, the whole family can participate in making creative and delicious foods.

What Kinds of Foods Can Be Dehydrated with The Nesco SnackMaster?

Because the Nesco SnackMaster is designed to be so versatile, you can dehydrate almost anything. From fruits and meat to herbs and crackers, the SnackMaster is designed to dehydrate anything, fast and consistently. Our fun and unique recipes will teach you the basics of dehydrating all types of different foods which can then be eaten as snack or added to other foods to create tasty dishes the whole family will love. And you can even use your SnackMaster to make non-food items such as dried flowers and potpourri. Once you start using your Nesco SnackMaster you will be amazed at how many different things you can make!

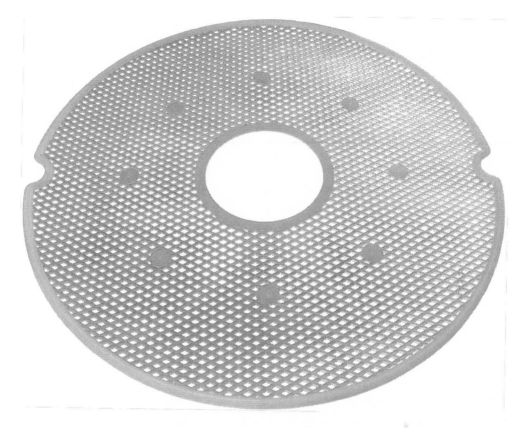

Helpful Accessories for Amazing Results

Your Nesco SnackMaster comes with everything you need to get started right away, but let's discuss how to use the unique accessories. If you are making dehydrated fruits which tend to be sticky, you will want to use the Nesco Clean-A-Screens which allow you to remove your dried fruit items easier than if they are placed directly on the rack. The Clean-A-Screens also come in handy when it's time for clean up because they are easy to remove from the machine. Your Nesco SnackMaster also allows you to purchase additional trays which can be used to expand the SnackMaster for extra capacity. So, if you want to make an extra-large batch of fruit leather or jerky, all you have to do is pop in extra trays and dehydrate to your heart's content. Best of all, the SnackMaster's accessories are inexpensive, durable, and very easy to use.

Use Your Nesco SnackMaster to Save Money!

These days, everyone is looking to save money when it comes to food, and the Nesco SnackMaster is the perfect way to stretch your food budget. Much like ancient humans from thousands of years ago, people today are concerned with food spoilage. Did you know that about half of all produce grown in the United States every year is thrown away because of spoilage? That's 60 million tons of food that would have been worth $160 billion! And millions of tons of meat are also wasted because they sit on store shelves for too long. That's a lot of money wasted every year on spoiled food. Imagine having a way to preserve that food while retaining almost all of the nutrients. Well, that's exactly what your Nesco SnackMaster does. Your foods will last longer while still being delicious and nutritious. And best of all, you won't waste money on spoiled food.

The Amazing Health Benefits of Using the Nesco SnackMaster

One of the best aspects of the Nesco SnackMaster is that, unlike other food preservation methods like canning, dehydrating doesn't destroy vital nutrients. And because your SnackMaster is the perfect way to preserve healthy foods like fruits, vegetables, and lean meats, it is the perfect way to encourage healthy eating habits. Two of the growing problems in many countries, including the United States, are obesity and diabetes. The cause of both of these problems is eating too much added sugar, much of which is found in processed snack foods. Your Nesco SnackMaster allows you to prepare snacks without added sugar because you get to control the ingredients. You can also eat healthy by making jerkies with lean meat and even fish. Since kids crave sweets, keeping them away from processed foods and candy can be difficult, but kids love the tasty and unique treats you can create with the SnackMaster. You might even find they prefer these healthy treats to store bought treats. And because the SnackMaster is so easy to use, the kids can help prepare their own snacks and come up with new and fun recipes.

3

HOW TO USE YOUR NESCO SNACKMASTER

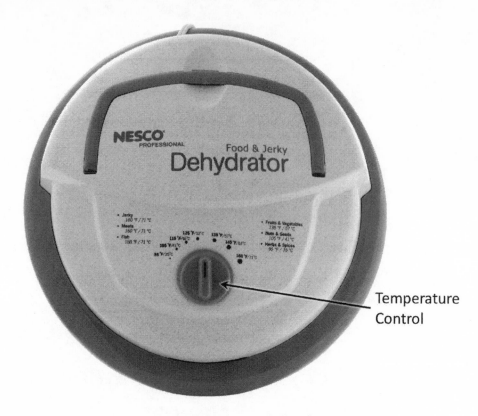

Temperature
Control

Get Started in Two Minutes with This Easy Guide

Setting up your Nesco SnackMaster really couldn't be easier. When you're ready to dehydrate, place the SnackMaster on a flat surface like a kitchen counter or table. Your SnackMaster requires at least five trays to function, but you can add up to seven trays if you are making a large batch. Then, simply place the cover on the top tray, install the blower, and turn the trays slightly to lock them into place. Before getting started, make sure your SnackMaster is plugged in with the power switched to "On". And that's it! You are now ready to start dehydrating.

Master the Temperature Settings in No Time

Your Nesco SnackMaster only has one control which allows you to set the temperature. Because the SnackMaster allows you to dry a wide variety of food, you will want to use different temperatures to achieve the best results. For fruits and vegetables, use a setting between 130F and 140F. This will allow you to thoroughly dehydrate the food without cooking away the valuable nutrients. For things like meat and fish you will want to use your SnackMaster's highest setting because you want to make sure to avoid any bacteria forming on your food. Fat rich foods like nuts and seeds need to be cooked at lower temperatures between 90F and 100F because their oil will take on an unpleasant taste if dried at higher temperature. You will also want to use these lower temperature settings for things like dried herbs or flowers. Otherwise, you risk losing their delicate flavors and aromas.

FRUITS & VEGETABLES

Use a setting between 130°F
(54.4°C) and 140°F (50°C)

MEAT & FISH

Use your SnackMaster's highest
setting

NUTS & SEEDS

Use a setting between 90°F
(32.2°C) and 100°F (37.7°C)

Prepare Your Food for Dehydration

In our recipes section, we will go into more depth about how to prepare specific foods, and there are many options to choose from. Meats benefit from marinating before dehydrating to maximize flavor and improve texture. Fruits can be sliced and dried whole or made into a variety of different purees that will give you a fruit leather when dehydrated. Items like fresh herbs and flowers require little to no preparation because you will want to maintain their unique, robust flavors.

Important Safety Tips for Your Nesco SnackMaster

As we've mentioned, the Nesco SnackMaster is one of the safest appliances in your kitchen. So safe, even the kids can get in on the dehydrating fun. The source of heat and air circulation is the blower. When cleaning your SnackMaster, make sure the blower is never submerged in water as this can damage the blower motor. When you have finished using your SnackMaster make sure to always unplug it, and make sure the plug and cord are not damaged before using. Because all food dehydrators are different, make sure to only use parts and accessories made specifically for the Nesco SnackMaster. Using other parts may result in damage to your SnackMaster. When using the SnackMaster with children, make sure they are properly supervised while using the temperature controls and power cord. For best results, never use your SnackMaster near a heat source such as an oven or stove. This can cause damage to the unit.

How to Clean and Store Your Nesco SnackMaster

Cleaning and storing your SnackMaster really couldn't be easier. Before you use your SnackMaster for the first time, make sure to wash the trays with soap and water. You may wash the trays in the dishwasher, but make sure to remove them from the dishwasher prior to the drying cycles because the high heat can damage them. Never put the blower in the dishwasher or submerge in water. To clean the blower, use a damp cloth, and make sure the air vents are not obstructed by anything. Otherwise the airflow into the SnackMaster may not be strong enough to work efficiently. After use, make sure to thoroughly clean the trays to remove all traces of food.

The Absolute Best Ways to Safely Store Your Dehydrated Foods

Once you've used your Nesco SnackMaster it's time to store those dried foods. Since you may use your SnackMaster quite often, you may find it helpful to label your foods. Simply choose Zip-lock bags, which you can write on with permanent marker. For easy reference, label with the type of food and the date you made it. Then there's no guessing about how old the food is. To store your foods for the maximum amount of time, try to always choose cool dark places. This will increase the shelf life of your food and ensure that the valuable vitamins and nutrients do not degrade with time. If possible, store your dried food in the refrigerator or freezer, but a cool dark cabinet will work well too. To minimize the possibility of insects invading your home, try to wrap and freeze all fruits with skin for forty-eight hours before defrosting and eating.

4

PRO TIPS

Use Your Dehydrator for Aromatherapy

Many people find aromatherapy to be a soothing and relaxing way of dealing with stress. Did you know you can use your Nesco SnackMaster as an aromatherapy tool? Simply pour a small quantity of water into a plastic or ceramic dish and add a few drops of your favorite essential oil. Turn the SnackMaster up to high heat, and as the water evaporates it will evenly distribute the soothing scent around your home. Always make sure to wash the SnackMaster thoroughly after using for aromatherapy. Otherwise the fragrant oils may find their way into your food.

You Can Use Your Nesco SnackMaster As A Humidifier!

During hot dry summers or cold dry winters, having a humidifier is a great way to keep your skin and nasal passages hydrated, but many humidifiers are large and cumbersome. To use your Nesco SnackMaster as an easy humidifier, simply place water in several containers which will fit inside the trays of the SnackMaster. Turn the unit to high heat and the water will quickly begin evaporating. Since the evaporation process is gradual, the air in your home will absorb the moisture more evenly and completely. For best results, use distilled water which has had the minerals removed.

How to Keep Food from Sticking to Your Nesco SnackMaster

Food sticking to dehydrator trays most commonly happens when drying pureed fruit because of the high sugar content. There are three quick and easy ways to prevent this from happening. First, be sure to use the fruit roll sheets which are provided with your SnackMaster. The smooth surface is designed to help avoid food sticking. You can also apply a very small amount of vegetable oil to the fruit roll sheets which will make removing the fruit rolls much easier. Lastly, make sure your fruit is properly dehydrated prior to removing it from the tray. When you look at your dehydrated fruit, there should not be any sticky or wet looking areas on the fruit. To ensure even dehydration, you will want to make sure the fruit puree is evenly distributed and not more than 1/4 inch thick.

Speed Up Dehydration Times for Fruits and Vegetables

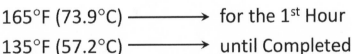

165°F (73.9°C) ⟶ for the 1st Hour

135°F (57.2°C) ⟶ until Completed

How to Speed Up Dehydration Times

For certain food, like jerkies, you will want to use the highest possible temperature setting at all times to avoid the formation of harmful bacteria. However, for fruits and vegetables, you can speed up your results by starting the dehydration at a higher heat for a short period of time. Fruits are typically dehydrated at a temperature of 130F to 140F for between four and eight hours. To speed things up a bit, start dehydrating at 165F for the first hour and then reset the temperature to 135F. This can help speed up the process by one to two hours depending on what you are dehydrating, and it should not have an effect on the flavor or nutritional value.

How to Guarantee Consistent Results for Every Batch!

The key to consistent results is even thickness. Whether you are dehydrating fruits, vegetables, or meats, you will get the best results if you make sure all of your ingredients are the same thickness. When slicing meat to make into jerky, try to make sure to cut all of the slices an identical thickness. When you are slicing fruit, try to cut your slices as uniformly as possible. Items like fruit rolls will come out best if you make sure to spread the puree evenly and not more that 1/4 inch thick. Doing this should cut down on batches where some of the food is perfectly dehydrated while the rest is either overly dried or still a bit too moist.

Cut Down on Food Waste with Your Nesco SnackMaster

Your Nesco SnackMaster is a powerful way to cut down on the problem of food waste. As we've mentioned, just in the United States alone we waste $160 billion every year because of spoilage. One of the best ways to stretch your food dollar every month is by not wasting food you've already paid for. The SnackMaster allows you to purchase perishable foods like meat, fruits, and vegetables and stretch their shelf life a long way. Those bananas that once turned brown in a week, can now last for months as healthy banana chips. Extra meat that might have been thrown away can now be made into jerky which will still be edible and delicious for a long time. Dehydrating food isn't just a great way to make fun and delicious snacks and meals, it's also a responsible choice for your family and the whole planet. So, let's get started by exploring one hundred amazing recipes which are sure to be a hit with your friends and family.

5

JERKY

Basic Beef Jerky

Whether it's for hitting the trails on a camping trip or just a healthy snack at home, this classic jerky recipe is sure to please your friends and family.

Prep time: 2 hours | Cook time: 4 hours | Servings: 6

Ingredients:

2 lbs. lean beef, cut into 1/8-inch-thick strips.

1/3 cup soy sauce

2 teaspoons liquid smoke

1 tablespoon brown sugar

1 teaspoon onion powder

1 tablespoon salt

2 teaspoons black pepper

Instructions:

1. In a large bowl, combine the beef, soy sauce, liquid smoke, brown sugar, onion powder, salt and pepper. Stir well and allow to marinate for two hours.

2. Remove beef strips from the bowl and wipe off excess marinade. Place the strips on a cutting board and pound with a mallet until strips are flat.

3. Place the strips on the racks of your Nesco SnackMaster and set to 165F. Dehydrate for 4 hours or until completely dried.

Nutritional Info: Calories: 297, Sodium: 2062 mg, Dietary Fiber: 0.3 g, Fat: 3.6 g, Carbs: 3.3 g, Protein: 46.9 g.

All-Natural Chicken Jerky

Great for people and pets, this all-natural chicken jerky is a perfect, protein packed snack that you can take wherever you go.

Prep time: 1 hour | Cook time: 6 hours | Servings: 6

Ingredients:

2 lbs. chicken breast tenders, cut into thin strips

1/2 cup soy sauce

2 teaspoons lemon juice

1/2 teaspoon ground ginger

1/2 teaspoon garlic powder

Instructions:

1. In a large bowl, combine the soy sauce, lemon juice, ginger, and garlic powder. Stir to combine and add the chicken. Marinate for one hour.

2. Remove chicken from the bowl and remove excess marinade. Place the strips on the racks of your Nesco SnackMaster. Set your SnackMaster to 145F and dehydrate for 6 hours.

3. Remove from the dehydrator and allow to cool before eating.

Nutritional Info: Calories: 137, Sodium: 145 mg, Dietary Fiber: 1.4 g, Fat: 4.8 g, Carbs: 10.2 g, Protein: 13.2 g.

Bacon Jerky

Who doesn't love bacon? This unique recipe will show you how to prepare regular bacon for long lasting and delicious results using your Nesco SnackMaster.

Prep time: 15 minutes | Cook time: 5 hours | Servings: 4

Ingredients:

1 lb. thick cut bacon

1 teaspoon black pepper

1 tablespoon brown sugar

1 teaspoon chili powder

Instructions:

1. Place the strips of bacon on baking sheets. In a small bowl, combine the pepper, sugar, and chili powder.

2. Season the bacon strips with the spice blend and allow to sit for 10 minutes.

3. Set your SnackMaster to 165F and arrange the bacon on the racks. Dehydrate for 5 hours.

4. Make sure all of the bacon is evenly dehydrated before removing from the racks.

Nutritional Info: Calories: 38, Sodium: 117 mg, Dietary Fiber: 0.4 g, Fat: 2.1 g, Carbs: 3 g, Protein: 1.9 g.

Turkey Jerky

A perfect, healthy alternative to traditional beef jerky, this amazing turkey jerky is great for snack at home or one the go. And your Nesco SnackMaster makes it so effortless, you'll never buy turkey jerky again.

Prep time: 2 hours | Cook time: 5 hours | Servings: 6

Ingredients:

2 lbs. boneless turkey breast

1/3 cup soy sauce

2 tablespoons brown sugar

1 tablespoon Worcestershire sauce

1/2 teaspoon onion powder

1 teaspoon black pepper

Instructions:

1. Slice the turkey breast into long thin strips, and pound flat with a mallet.

2. In a large bowl, combine the soy sauce, brown sugar, Worcestershire sauce, onion powder, and pepper. Add the turkey strips and allow to marinate for 2 hours.

3. Set your Nesco SnackMaster to 165F and place the turkey strips evenly on the racks.

4. Dehydrate for 5 to 6 hours or until the strips are fully dehydrated.

Nutritional Info: Calories: 180, Sodium: 842 mg, Dietary Fiber: 1 g, Fat: 2.5 g, Carbs: 11.3 g, Protein: 26.8 g.

Wild Salmon Jerky

This healthy treat is packed with flavor and nutrition. By dehydrating you lock in the omega-3 oils which are beneficial for heart health.

Prep time: 2 hours | Cook time: 4 hours | Servings: 4

Ingredients:

1 lb. wild salmon filets, sliced into thin strips

1/2 cup soy sauce

1 teaspoon liquid smoke

1 tablespoon lemon juice

1 teaspoon black pepper

Instructions:

1. In a large bowl or zip-lock bag, combine the salmon strips, soy sauce, liquid smoke, lemon juice, and pepper. Place in the refrigerator and marinate for 2 hours.

2. Remove salmon from the marinade and wipe off excess marinade.

3. Set your Nesco SnackMaster to 145F and lay the salmon strips evenly on the racks.

4. Dehydrate for 4 hours. Remove from the racks and allow to cool completely before storing.

Nutritional Info: Calories: 67, Sodium: 896 mg, Dietary Fiber: 0.4 g, Fat: 3.1 g, Carbs: 2.9 g, Protein: 7.3 g.

Spicy Beef Jerky

If you want to kick your classic beef jerky up a notch, this recipe will show you how to get perfectly balanced flavors with a bit of a kick.

Prep time: 2 hours | Cook time: 5 hours | Servings: 8

Ingredients:

2 lbs. lean beef, cut into thin strips.

1/2 cup soy sauce

1/2 cup Worcestershire sauce

2 tablespoons brown sugar

1 tablespoon onion powder

1 teaspoon garlic powder

1 teaspoon cayenne pepper, or 2 teaspoons if you want it really spicy

1 teaspoon liquid smoke

Instructions:

1. Using a mallet, pound the beef strips until flat. In a large bowl combine the soy sauce, Worcestershire sauce, sugar, onion powder, garlic powder, cayenne pepper, and liquid smoke.

2. Place the beef strips in the bowl and allow to marinate for 2 hours.

3. Set your Nesco SnackMaster to 165F. and lay the marinated strips on the racks. Dehydrate for 5 hours.

4. Make sure the strips are completely dehydrated before removing them from the dehydrator.

Nutritional Info: Calories: 248, Sodium: 963 mg, Dietary Fiber: 0.3 g, Fat: 7.1 g, Carbs: 7.5 g, Protein: 35.6 g.

Smokey Pork Jerky

Pork jerky isn't as common as beef or turkey, but it has a delicate flavor and texture which makes it perfect for dehydrating in your Nesco SnackMaster.

Prep time: 1 hour | Cook time: 6 hours | Servings: 8

Ingredients:

2 lbs. pork loin

1 tablespoon soy sauce

1 salt

1 teaspoon black pepper

1/2 teaspoon onion powder

1 tablespoon brown sugar

1 teaspoon liquid smoke

Instructions:

1. Slice the pork into thin strips about 1/4 inch thick. In a large bowl, combine the soy sauce, salt, black pepper, liquid smoke, onion powder, and brown sugar. Add the pork strips to the bowl and allow to marinate for 1 hour.

2. Remove the pork strips from the bowl and remove excess marinade. Lay the pork strips evenly on the racks of your Nesco SnackMaster and set to 165F. Dehydrate for 6 hours.

3. When the pork strips are completely dehydrated remove from the dehydrator and cool before storing.

Nutritional Info: Calories: 281, Sodium: 203 mg, Dietary Fiber: 0.1 g, Fat: 15.8 g, Carbs: 1.6 g, Protein: 31.2 g.

Ham Jerky

Ham already has a robust flavor, and this flavor is only enhanced by dehydrating with your Nesco SnackMaster. This great snack is perfect for enjoying anywhere!

Prep time: 1 hour | Cook time: 4 hours | Servings: 4

Ingredients:

1 lb. sliced ham

4 tablespoons soy sauce

4 tablespoons water

1 teaspoon pepper

1/2 teaspoon onion powder

Instructions:

1. In a large bowl combine the soy sauce, water, pepper, and onion powder. Add the ham slices and turn to coat. Allow the ham to marinate for 1 hour.

2. Remove the ham from the bowl and remove excess marinade. Set your Nesco SnackMaster to 165F and place the ham strips evenly on the racks.

3. Dehydrate for 4 hours and make sure the ham is evenly dehydrated before removing from the racks.

Nutritional Info: Calories: 196, Sodium: 831 mg, Dietary Fiber: 1.8 g, Fat: 9.8 g, Carbs: 6.1 g, Protein: 19.9 g.

Cranberry Turkey Jerky

This fun takes on classic turkey jerky is a perfect pre-Thanksgiving snack the whole family will love. The tart, earthy flavors of cranberry pair perfectly with lean turkey breast.

Prep time: 3 hours | Cook time: 5 hours | Servings: 8

Ingredients:

2 lbs. turkey breast, cut into thin strips

1/2 cup orange juice

2 tablespoons brown sugar

1 cup cranberry sauce

2 tablespoons salt

Instructions:

1. In a large bowl, combine the orange juice, brown sugar, cranberry sauce, and salt. Mix well into an even paste. Add the turkey breast strips and mix well. Allow to marinate for 3 hours.

2. Set your Nesco SnackMaster to 165F. Remove the turkey strips from the bowl and remove excess marinade. Lay the turkey strips on the racks of your SnackMaster and dehydrate for 5 hours.

3. Make sure the jerky is completely dehydrated before removing from the racks.

Nutritional Info: Calories: 141, Sodium: 896 mg, Dietary Fiber: 1.1 g, Fat: 1.9 g, Carbs: 9.8 g, Protein: 19.5 g.

Korean Beef Jerky

This fun takes on beef jerky uses the flavors of Korean BBQ to create a jerky that is bursting with interesting and robust flavors.

Prep time: 6 hours | Cook time: 5 hours | Servings: 4

Ingredients:

1 lb. lean beef, cut into thin strips

1/2 cup soy sauce

3 tablespoons mirin

1 tablespoon brown sugar

1 teaspoon garlic, finely minced

3 tablespoons sesame seeds

1 teaspoon fresh ginger, grated

Instructions:

1. In a large zipper lock bag, combine the soy sauce, mirin, brown sugar, garlic, and ginger. Place the beef strips in the bowl and allow to marinate for 6 hours.

2. Set your Nesco SnackMaster to 165F. Remove the beef strips from the bowl and remove excess marinade. Place the beef strips on the racks of your Nesco SnackMaster and sprinkle with sesame seeds.

3. Dehydrate for 5 hours. Before removing the beef strips from the racks make sure they are completely dehydrated.

Nutritional Info: Calories: 296, Sodium: 971 mg, Dietary Fiber: 1.1 g, Fat: 10.5 g, Carbs: 12 g, Protein: 37.7 g.

6

POWDERS AND LEATHERS

Apricot Fruit Leather

This classic fruit leather is delicious and packed with nutrients. Best of all, you can avoid chemicals often found in store bought fruit leather.

Prep time: 20 minutes | Cook time: 6 hours | Servings: 12

Ingredients:

2 cups apricot, pitted

1/2 cup sugar

2 teaspoons lemon juice

Instructions:

1. In a medium saucepan combine the apricot, sugar, and lemon juice. Cook until sugar has dissolved, and the apricots are beginning to break down.

2. Pour the mixture into a blender and blend until smooth.

3. Place Clean-A-Screens on the racks of your Nesco SnackMaster. Pour the apricot puree onto the screens and use a spatula to spread the puree evenly about an 1/8-inch-thick.

4. Set your SnackMaster to 140F dehydrate for 6 hours. Make sure leather has completely dehydrate before using a spatula to remove from the screens.

Nutritional Info: Calories: 44, Sodium: 1 mg, Dietary Fiber: 0.5 g, Fat: 0.2 g, Carbs: 11.2 g, Protein: 0.3 g.

Strawberry Passion Fruit Leather

This tart and robust fruit leather is extra complex thanks to the combination of fresh strawberries and sweet passions fruit syrup.

Prep time: 10 minutes | Cook time: 6 hours | Servings: 6

Ingredients:

2 cups fresh strawberries, stems removed

2 tablespoons passion fruit syrup

1 cup applesauce

Instructions:

1. Place the strawberries, passion fruit syrup, and applesauce into a blender and puree until smooth.

2. Place Clean-A-Screens on the racks of your Nesco SnackMaster and pour the puree onto the screens. Use a spatula to evenly distribute the puree so it is about 1/8-inch-thick.

3. Set your SnackMaster to 140F and dehydrate for 6 hours. Make sure your leather is completely dehydrated and not sticky before removing from the screens.

Nutritional Info: Calories: 46, Sodium: 1 mg, Dietary Fiber: 1.5 g, Fat: 0.2 g, Carbs: 11.5 g, Protein: 0.4 g.

Blueberry Flax Seed Leather

This delicious fruit leather is packed with antioxidant powers of blueberries and flax seed for a treat that is both tasty and full of valuable nutrients. And they taste so good, the kids won't even know they're eating healthy.

Prep time: 10 minutes | Cook time: 4 hours | Servings: 4

Ingredients:

1 banana

2 cups blueberries

1 tablespoon ground flax seeds

1 tablespoon lemon juice

Instructions;

1. In a blender, combine the banana, blueberries, flax seeds, and lemon juice. Blend until smooth.

2. Place Clean-A-Screens on the racks of your SnackMaster and set to 115F.

3. Pour the blueberry puree onto the screens and use a spatula to even spread the puree about 1/8 inch thick.

4. Dehydrate for 4 hours and make sure the leather is completely dehydrated and not sticky before removing from the sheets.

Nutritional Info: Calories: 78, Sodium: 2 mg, Dietary Fiber: 3 g, Fat: 0.9 g, Carbs: 17.8 g, Protein: 1.2 g.

Plum Fruit Leather

This sweet and tart leather is a great way to use plums. The natural sugars and acids create a perfect blend of flavors that is sure to please the whole family.

Prep time: 20 minutes | Cook time: 8 hours | Servings: 12

Ingredients:

6 purple or red plums split and pitted

2 tablespoons lemon juice

2 teaspoons ground cinnamon

1/4 cup water

Instructions:

1. Place the plums and water in a pot and simmer until the plums begin to break down, about 10 to 15 minutes. When the plums are soft, pour into a blender and blend until smooth.

2. Add the lemon juice and cinnamon and blend.

3. Place Clean-A-Screens on the racks of your SnackMaster and set to 140F.

4. Pour the puree onto the screens and use a spatula to spread the puree evenly, about 1/8 inch thick.

5. Dehydrate for 8 hours. Make sure the leather is completely dehydrated and not sticky before removing from the screens.

Nutritional Info: Calories: 6, Sodium: 1 mg, Dietary Fiber: 0.3 g, Fat: 0.1 g, Carbs: 1.5 g, Protein: 0.1 g.

Simple Apple Leather

This basic apple leather is so simple anyone in the family can make it. And because there is no added sugar, you can feel good about serving it as a snack for the whole family.

Prep time: 5 minutes | Cook time: 6 hours | Servings: 12

Ingredients:

8 cups applesauce   1 3oz. box sugar free Jell-O

Instructions:

1.   In a large bowl, combine the applesauce and Jell-O. Place Clean-A-Screens on the racks of your SnackMaster and pour the puree onto the screens. Use a spatula to evenly spread the puree about 1/8 inch thick.

2.   Set your SnackMaster to 140F and dehydrate for 6 hours. Make sure the leather is completely dehydrated and not sticky before removing from the screens.

Nutritional Info: Calories: 103, Sodium: 187 mg, Dietary Fiber: 2 g, Fat: 0.1 g, Carbs: 18.4 g, Protein: 3.6 g.

Tomato Powder

This easy to prepare flavor powder is a great way to add the robust flavor of concentrated tomatoes to season dishes and sauces.

Prep time: 10 minutes | Cook time: 4 hours | Servings: 24

Ingredients:

3 lbs. fresh tomatoes

Instructions:

1. Slice the tomatoes about an 1/8 inch thick. Place Clean-A-Screens on the racks of your Nesco SnackMaster.

2. Lay the tomato slices on the screens in a single layer so they do not touch. Set your Nesco SnackMaster to 150F and dehydrate for 4 hours.

3. When tomatoes are completely dehydrated, transfer them to a blender, and pulse until a fine powder form. Store the powder in a jar or zip-lock bag.

Nutritional Info: Calories: 10, Sodium: 3 mg, Dietary Fiber: 0.7 g, Fat: 0.1 g, Carbs: 2.2 g, Protein: 0.5 g.

Mirepoix Powder

Mirepoix is a mixture of onion, carrot, and celery which acts as a base for soups, stews, and a multitude of sauces. This powdered version allows you to add this unique flavor to anything without having to make a new batch every time you cook.

Prep time: 20 minutes | Cook time: 6 hours | Servings: 24

Ingredients:

2 yellow onions, thinly sliced

3 carrots, sliced into thin rounds

3 stalks celery, cut into thin slices

Instructions:

1. Place Clean-A-Screens on the racks of your Nesco SnackMaster. On separate racks place layers of onion, carrot, and celery. Make sure they are even layers.

2. Set your SnackMaster to 150F and dehydrate for 6 hours.

3. When the vegetables are completely dehydrated, place them in a blender together. Blend until a fine powder form. Store the powder in jars and use as the base for many soups and sauces.

Nutritional Info: Calories: 7, Sodium: 7 mg, Dietary Fiber: 0.4 g, Fat: 0 g, Carbs: 1.7 g, Protein: 0.2 g.

Spicy Carrot Powder

This spicy vegetable powder is a great way to infuse concentrated flavor into many different dishes or try using it as a finishing condiment for a hint of carrot and heat.

Prep time: 15 minutes | Cook time: 6 hours | Servings: 12

Ingredients:

6 large carrots, peeled

2 jalapeno peppers, sliced

1 tablespoon salt

Instructions:

1. Cut the carrots into chunks and place in a food processor. Pulse until the carrots are roughly chopped but not a puree.

2. Place Clean-A-Screens on the racks of your Nesco SnackMaster and use all but one rack for the carrots. Make sure the carrots are in thin even layers not thicker than 1/4 inch.

3. Use one rack for the jalapeño peppers. Set your SnackMaster to 150F and dehydrate for 6 hours or until the carrots are completely dry.

4. Transfer the dried carrots and jalapenos to a blender and blend until a fine powder form. Store in jars or zip-lock bags.

Nutritional Info: Calories: 16, Sodium: 667 mg, Dietary Fiber: 1 g, Fat: 0 g, Carbs: 3.7 g, Protein: 0.3 g.

Homemade Chili Powder

Dried chilies are a great way to add robust spice to any dish, but chilies lose their potency over time. To ensure you have the most flavorful chili powder, use your Nesco SnackMaster to make your own at home.

Prep time: 15 minutes | Cook time: 5 to 6 hours | Servings: 24

Ingredients:

12 red chili peppers

Instructions:

1. Place Clean-A-Screens on the racks of your Nesco SnackMaster.

2. Carefully slice the chili peppers into thin strips. Note: The amount of heat in your chili powder will depend on how much pith and seed you allow to stay with the peppers.

3. If you want super-hot powder keep the seeds and pith. For less spicy powder discard most of the seeds and pith.

4. Lay the peppers (and seeds and pith if desired) on the screens and set your SnackMaster to 115F.

5. Dehydrate for 5 to 6 hours or until the peppers are completely dried. Transfer the contents of your SnackMaster to a blender and pulse until a rough powder form. Store in jars or zip-lock bags.

Nutritional Info: Calories: 1, Sodium: 0 mg, Dietary Fiber: 0.1 g, Fat: 0 g, Carbs: 0.2 g, Protein: 0 g.

Green Onion Powder

Green onions are a great way to add flavor to many dishes and soups, but if you want to have their unique flavor without pieces of green onion, you can use this flavorful powder to enhance your dishes.

Prep time: 10 minutes | Cook time: 12 hours | Servings: 12

Ingredients:

1/2 lb. green onions.

Instructions:

1. Wash the green onions and cut off the white bottoms. Slice the green parts into 1/2-inch pieces.

2. Place Clean-A-Screens on the racks of your SnackMaster and set to 115F. Evenly distribute the chopped green onion on the screens forming a single layer.

3. Dehydrate for 12 hours or until all of the onions are completely dried. Transfer the contents to a blender and pulse until you have a fine powder. Store in jars or a zip-lock bag.

Nutritional Info: Calories: 6, Sodium: 3 mg, Dietary Fiber: 0.5 g, Fat: 0 g, Carbs: 1.4 g, Protein: 0.4 g.

7

BREADS, CRACKERS, and CHIPS

Vegan Bread

This healthy alternative to regular bread is perfect for vegan or gluten free diets and packs plenty of earthy flavors the whole family will love.

Prep time: 30 minutes | Cook time: 6 hours | Servings: 6

Ingredients:

1 head cauliflower

1 teaspoon turmeric

2 tablespoons flax seed

1/2 cup psyllium husk

1/2 cup brewer's yeast

4 large zucchinis

salt and black pepper

Instructions:

1. Place cauliflower and zucchini in a food processor and pulse until they form a paste. Add the turmeric, flax seeds, psyllium, yeast, and a pinch of salt and black pepper. Pulse again until all ingredients are thoroughly combined.

2. Place Clean-A-Screens on the racks of your Nesco SnackMaster. Form the mixture into slices about 1/2-inch-thick, and place on the screens.

3. Set your SnackMaster to 150F and dehydrate for 6 hours. The bread should not be completely dry. One side should be slightly soft.

Nutritional Info: Calories: 219, Sodium: 156 mg, Dietary Fiber: 45.1 g, Fat: 1.9 g, Carbs: 61.6 g, Protein: 10.1 g.

Fluffy Dinner Rolls

These creative dinner rolls are packed with complex flavors that pair well with many different meals and are perfect for those looking for a gluten free alternative to regular bread.

Prep time: 15 minutes | Cook time: 7 hours | Servings: 6

Ingredients:

2 cups almond flour

1 cup psyllium

3 tablespoons ground flax seeds

1 tablespoon onion powder

2 teaspoons garlic powder

1 tablespoon lemon juice

1 teaspoon salt

1/3 cup water

Instructions:

1. In a large bowl, combine the flour, psyllium, flax seeds, onion powder, garlic powder, lemon juice, salt, and water. Mix well until combined.

2. Form the mixture into 6 round rolls.

3. Place Clean-A-Screens on the racks of your SnackMaster. Place the rolls on the screens so they are not touching.

4. Dehydrate at 145F for one hour, then lower the temperature to 110F for the remaining 6 hours. Remove from the screens and serve warm or allow to cool before storing.

Nutritional Info: Calories: 319, Sodium: 620 mg, Dietary Fiber: 77.4 g, Fat: 7.1 g, Carbs: 95.2 g, Protein: 3.5 g.

Herb and Almond Crackers

These flavorful crackers are great with cheese or dip, or on their own as a healthy and tasty snack any time of day.

Prep time: 10 minutes | Cook time: 12 hours | Servings: 6

Ingredients:

2 cups almonds

1/2 cup ground flax seeds

1/4 cup brewer's yeast

3/4 cups water

2 tablespoons fresh rosemary, finely chopped

1 teaspoon salt

1/2 teaspoon black pepper

Instructions:

1. In a food processor, combine the almonds, flax seed, yeast, salt, and pepper. Pulse until well combined.

2. Slowly add the water while continuing to pulse until a paste form.

3. Place Clean-A-Screens on the racks of your SnackMaster and spread a thin layer of the paste onto each screen. Set your SnackMaster to 115F and dehydrate for 12 hours or until the crackers are crispy. Remove from the screens and break into small pieces to serve.

Nutritional Info: Calories: 260, Sodium: 396 mg, Dietary Fiber: 8.7 g, Fat: 19.3 g, Carbs: 13.3 g, Protein: 11.6 g.

Carrot Crackers

These light vegetable crackers are a light and delicious snack or use in place of regular crackers when entertaining.

Prep time: 20 minutes | Cook time: 12 hours | Servings: 12

Ingredients:

6 large carrots, peeled

1/2 cup ground flax seeds

1 tomato, diced

Juice from 1 lemon

1/2 cup sesame seeds

1/2 cup chia seeds

3/4 cups water

Instructions:

1. In a food processor, combine the carrots, flax seeds, tomato, lemon juice, and water, and pulse until a paste form. Add the chia seeds, and sesame seeds and stir to combine.

2. Place Clean-A-Screens on the racks of your Nesco SnackMaster. Spread the paste evenly on the screens about 1/4 inch thick.

3. Set your SnackMaster to 105F and dehydrate for 12 hours. Remove the crackers from the SnackMaster and allow to cool completely. The crackers will become crispy as they cool.

Nutritional Info: Calories: 122, Sodium: 29 mg, Dietary Fiber: 6.2 g, Fat: 7.4 g, Carbs: 10.8 g, Protein: 3.9 g.

Sweet Potato Chips

These sweet potato chips are so easy to make and are a great replacement for traditional potato chips.

Prep time: 10 minutes | Cook time: 12 to 14 hours | Servings: 6

Ingredients:

2 large sweet potatoes

2 teaspoons coconut oil, melted

2 teaspoons salt

Instructions:

1. Using a mandolin, slice the potatoes into thin rounds. In a large bowl, combine the potato slices, salt, and coconut oil and toss to coat.

2. Place Clean-A-Screens on the racks of your Nesco SnackMaster and place the potato slices on the screens in a single layer.

3. Set your SnackMaster to 125F and dehydrate for 12 to 14 hours or until the potato slices are crisp. Remove from the screens and store in a cool dry place if not using immediately.

Nutritional Info: Calories: 13, Sodium: 775 mg, Dietary Fiber: 0 g, Fat: 1.5 g, Carbs: 0.1 g, Protein: 0 g.

Nuts and Seeds Crackers

These fun homemade crackers are the perfect way to get a big dose of nutrition in an easy to make snack. Once you've tried these dehydrated crackers, you'll wonder why you ever bought crackers at the store.

Prep time: 4 hours | Cook time: 24 hours | Servings: 20

Ingredients:

1 cup sunflower seeds

1 cup brazil nuts

1 cup almonds

2 tablespoons tomato paste

1 cup red bell pepper, minced

1 cup ground flax seed

1 tablespoon salt

Instructions:

1. In a large bowl of water, soak the sunflower seeds, brazil nuts, and almonds for 4 hours.

2. In a food processor, combine the sunflower seeds, brazil nuts, almonds, tomato paste, bell pepper, flax seed, and salt. Pulse until the paste is smooth.

3. Place Clean-A-Screens on the racks of your SnackMaster. Pour the paste onto the screens and use a spatula to spread the mixture evenly about 1/8 inch thick.

4. Set your SnackMaster to 115F and dehydrate for 24 hours.

Nutritional Info: Calories: 113, Sodium: 353 mg, Dietary Fiber: 2.9 g, Fat: 9.4 g, Carbs: 4.6 g, Protein: 3.5 g.

Crunch Green Bean Chips

The whole family will fall in love with these tasty and crunch green bean crisps. And best of all, since you control the ingredients, you are guaranteed the healthiest snack possible.

Prep time: 10 minutes | Cook time: 12 hours | Servings: 12

Ingredients:

3 lbs. fresh green beans

1/4 cup coconut oil, melted

1 tablespoon salt

Instructions:

1. In a large bowl, combine the green beans and oil and stir well to coat. Season with salt and stir again.

2. Place the green beans on the racks of your SnackMaster and set to 125F. Dehydrate for 12 hours or until the beans are completely dry and crispy.

3. Remove the green beans from the racks and store in a cool dry place.

Nutritional Info: Calories: 74, Sodium: 588 mg, Dietary Fiber: 3.9 g, Fat: 9.4 g, Carbs: 4.7 g, Protein: 2.1 g.

Eggplant Chips

Eggplants can be enjoyed in a variety of ways, but their complex, earthy tones are ideal for dehydration because the concentrated flavors are front and center.

Prep time: 15 minutes | Cook time: 5 to 6 hours | Servings: 6

Ingredients:

4 baby eggplants

3 tablespoons olive oil

1/2 teaspoon smoked paprika

1/2 teaspoon oregano

1/4 teaspoon cayenne pepper

2 tablespoons salt

Instructions:

1. Use a mandolin to slice the eggplant into thin rounds. In a large bowl, combine the eggplant slices olive oil, paprika, oregano, cayenne pepper, and salt.

2. Place the eggplant slices on the racks of your SnackMaster and set to 135F. Dehydrate for 5 to 6 hours or until eggplant slices are completely dried and crispy.

Nutritional Info: Calories: 153, Sodium: 938 mg, Dietary Fiber: 13.1 g, Fat: 7.7 g, Carbs: 21.7 g, Protein: 3.6 g.

Pumpkin Chips

These unique pumpkin chips are perfect for snacking in Autumn or any time of the year. You can also experiment with adding different seasonings to customize your chips.

Prep time: 10 minutes | Cook time: 18 hours | Servings: 6

Ingredients:

1 pumpkin

2 tablespoons coconut oil, melted

1 teaspoon cinnamon

1 teaspoon nutmeg

1 teaspoon salt

Instructions:

1. Remove the seeds, pulp, and skin from the pumpkin, and slice the pumpkin flesh into thin slices. Try to make the slices no more that 1/8 inch thick.

2. In a large bowl, combine the pumpkin slices, coconut oil, cinnamon, nutmeg, and salt. Stir well to coat.

3. Place the pumpkin slices on the racks of your SnackMaster and set to 125F. Dehydrated for 18 hours or until the slices are crispy.

Nutritional Info: Calories: 736, Sodium: 490 mg, Dietary Fiber: 59.5 g, Fat: 10.6 g, Carbs: 165.7 g, Protein: 22.5 g.

Zucchini Chips

The combination of natural zucchini flavor and bright citrus makes these chips an exciting and healthy alternative to traditional chips.

Prep time: 10 minutes | Cook time: 12 hours | Servings: 6

Ingredients:

4 zucchinis

Juice from 2 lemons

1 teaspoon salt

Instructions:

1. Using a mandolin, slice the zucchini into thin strips.

2. In a large bowl, combine the zucchini strips, lemon juice, and salt, and stir to coat.

3. Place the zucchini strips on the racks of your Nesco SnackMaster in a single layer. Set the SnackMaster to 115F and dehydrate for 12 hours or until the zucchini strips are crispy.

Nutritional Info: Calories: 25, Sodium: 401 mg, Dietary Fiber: 1.5 g, Fat: 0.3 g, Carbs: 5.8 g, Protein: 1.7 g.

8

HERBS and FLOWERS

Greek Herb Blend

This fragrant and delicious herb blend is perfect for seasoning salads and marinating meat. Dehydrating your own herb blends guarantees the freshest and boldest flavors.

Prep time: 5 minutes | Cook time: 24 hours | Servings: 24

Ingredients:

1 bunch fresh basil

1 bunch fresh oregano

1 bunch fresh rosemary

1 bunch fresh thyme

1/2 onion, minced

3 cloves garlic, minced

Instructions:

1. Wash and dry the fresh herbs and place a different herb on each rack of your Nesco SnackMaster.

2. Place a Clean-A-Screen on the remaining rack and place the onion on one side and the garlic on the other.

3. Set your SnackMaster to 115F and dehydrate for 24 hours.

4. When the herbs, garlic, and onion are all completely dry, transfer them to a blender and pulse until finely chopped and combined.

Nutritional Info: Calories: 4, Sodium: 0 mg, Dietary Fiber: 0.2 g, Fat: 0 g, Carbs: 0.6 g, Protein: 0.1 g.

Italian Herb Blend

This classic herb blend is an integral part of so many Italian dishes, from tomato sauces to meat seasonings and marinades, you will never run out of uses for this delicious blend.

Prep time: 10 minutes | Cook time: 24 hours | Servings: 24

Ingredients:

1 bunch fresh basil

1 bunch fresh oregano

1 bunch fresh rosemary

1 bunch fresh marjoram

1/2 bunch cilantro

1/2 bunch fresh thyme

Instructions:

1. Wash all of the herbs and remove the leaves from the stems. In a large bowl, combine all of the herbs, and mix well.

2. Place the herb mix on the racks of your Nesco SnackMaster and set to 115F. Dehydrate for 24 hours. Make sure all of the herbs are completely dried before removing them from the dehydrator.

3. When herbs are dried, pour them into a blender, and pulse until the herbs are chopped and well mixed. Store in jars or zipper lock bags.

Nutritional Info: Calories: 3, Sodium: 0 mg, Dietary Fiber: 0.4 g, Fat: 0.1g, Carbs: 0.6 g, Protein: 0.1 g.

Mint Leaves

This quick and easy method for drying mint leaves is perfect if you want to add the flavor of fresh mint to marinades, sauces, teas, or salads.

Prep time: 10 minutes | Cook time: 6 hours | Servings: 12

Ingredients:

2 bunches fresh peppermint or spearmint

Instructions:

1.   Remove the mint leaves from the stems and rinse well. Place the leaves on the rack of your Nesco SnackMaster and set to 150F. Dehydrate for 6 hours.

2.   Remove mint leaves from the racks and store in jars or zip-lock bags until ready to use.

Nutritional Info: Calories: 2, Sodium: 1 mg, Dietary Fiber: 0.3 g, Fat: 0 g, Carbs: 0.3 g, Protein: 0.1 g.

Dried Cilantro

Cilantro is a flavorful herb which appears in cooking from all over the world. This simple recipe for drying cilantro allows you to have the fresh flavor of cilantro on hand at all times.

Prep time: 10 minutes | Cook time: 3 hours | Servings: 12

Ingredients:

2 bunches fresh cilantro

Instructions:

1. You can dehydrate your cilantro with or without the stems; it's totally up to you. Rinse and dry the cilantro and place it in a single layer on the racks of your Nesco SnackMaster.

2. Set your SnackMaster to 110F and dehydrate for 3 hours. Remove the dried cilantro from the racks and store in jars or zip-lock bags until ready to use.

Nutritional Info: Calories: 0, Sodium: 1 mg, Dietary Fiber: 0 g, Fat: 0 g, Carbs: 0.1 g, Protein: 0 g.

Lemon Basil Blend

This innovative way of preparing dried basil makes a perfect addition to salads or as a seasoning for poultry and fish dishes.

Prep time: 15 minutes | Cook time: 12 hours | Servings: 24

Ingredients:

2 bunches fresh basil

juice from 1 lemon

Instructions:

1. Rinse and dry your basil and remove the leaves from the stems.

2. Place the basil leaves in a large bowl and sprinkle the lemon juice over them. Mix well until all of the leave is coated in lemon juice.

3. Place the basil in a single layer on the racks of your Nesco SnackMaster. Try to keep the leaves from touching.

4. Set your SnackMaster to 115F and dehydrate for 24 hours. When the basil is finished they should feel dry and not sticky.

5. Remove the basil from the racks and store in jars or zip-lock bags until ready to use.

Nutritional Info: Calories: 1, Sodium: 0 mg, Dietary Fiber: 0 g, Fat: 0 g, Carbs: 0.2 g, Protein: 0 g.

Dried Rose Petals

This fragrance of rose petals is a wonderful way to freshen up your home. This easy guide to dehydrating rose petals allows you to create long lasting dried flowers which retain their natural robust aromas.

Prep time: 15 minutes | Cook time: 4 to 5 hours

Ingredients:

Fresh rose petals from your choice of roses

Instructions:

---

1. Select the type of rose you would like to use. Different varieties have different aromas, and some are stronger and sweeter than others. For best results, only dehydrate one type of flower at a time because different types of roses require different drying times.

2. Remove the rose petals from the stems and place the petals on the rack of your Nesco SnackMaster in single layers.

3. Set your SnackMaster to 115F and dehydrate for 4 to 5 hours, or until the petals are completely dry. Your dried rose petals should retain their strong aromas for several months.

Apple Cinnamon Potpourri

This fragrant homemade potpourri is perfect for giving your home a flavor of Fall. Your Nesco SnackMaster ensures your potpourri will the freshest, most fragrant potpourri you've ever smelled.

Prep time: 15 minutes | Cook time: 12 hours

Ingredients:
-----

2 red delicious apples   *Juice from 1 lemon*
1 tablespoon ground cinnamon

Instructions:
-----

1.   Slice the apples into even slices around 1/8 inch thick. In a large bowl combine the apples and lemon juice. Stir well to make sure all of the apple slices are coated in lemon juice. Sprinkle in the cinnamon and stir again.

2.   Place the apple slices on the racks of your Nesco SnackMaster in a single layer so they are not touching.

3.   Set your SnackMaster to 150F and dehydrate for 12 hours. The apple slices should be completely dried and no longer sticky. Remove from the racks and place around the house or store in airtight jars until ready to use.

Citrus Potpourri

This potpourri is a great way to add freshness to your home with the simple yet robust flavors of fresh citrus and spices. Perfect for the winter holidays or any time of the year. It also makes a great, simple gift.

Prep time: 15 minutes | Cook time: 12 hours

Ingredients:

2 lemons

2 oranges

6 cinnamon sticks

3 tablespoons dried cloves

Instructions:

1. Slice the lemons and oranges between 1/8 and 1/4-inch-thick and place them on the racks of your Nesco SnackMaster in a single layer so the slices are not touching.

2. Set your SnackMaster to 150F and dehydrate for 12 hours. The citrus should be dry and firm to the touch and not sticky.

3. Remove the slices from the racks and divide among bowls or jars with equal amounts of cinnamon sticks and dried cloves.

Lavender Potpourri

Lavender has a wonderful fresh scent that always reminds you of walking through a garden in springtime. This easy to make lavender potpourri allows you to bring the delightful floral scent into your home whenever you want.

Prep time: 5 minutes | Cook time: 6 hours

Ingredients:

Fresh lavender   *Essential oils (optional)*

Instructions:

1. Collect lavender and trim them so there are several inches of stem below the flowers.

2. Place the flowers on the racks of your Nesco SnackMaster in a single layer. If using essential oils, sprinkle a few drops on the flowers before you start dehydrating.

3. Set your SnackMaster to 115F and dehydrate for 6 hours. Remove the flowers from the racks and place around the house, or store in airtight bags until ready to use.

Holiday Potpourri

The smell of this classic potpourri will automatically transport you to the holidays. Use it to put your family in a holiday mood or give it out as fun gifts. Making your own potpourri in your Nesco SnackMaster means you will always have the freshest most fragrant potpourri.

Prep time: 10 minutes | Cook time: 12 hours

Ingredients:

1 orange

1/2 cup fresh cranberries

6 cinnamon sticks

2 tablespoons dried cloves

1/4 cup whole nutmeg

1/4 dried star anise

Instructions:

1. Slice the orange into slices about 1/8 inch thick. Place the orange slices on all but one of the racks of your SnackMaster. On the remaining rack, place the cranberries.

2. Set your SnackMaster to 115F and dehydrate for 12 hours.

3. When the orange slices are dehydrated they will be firm and dry to the touch and no longer sticky.

4. Remove the orange slices and dried cranberries from the racks and, in a large bowl, combine them with the cinnamon sticks, cloves, nutmeg, and star anise.

5. Allow the mixture to sit, combined for several hours before dividing into jars or zip-lock bags.

9

TEAS

Strawberry Mint Tea

This fun takes on traditional black tea is packed with flavors thanks to the dehydrating power of you Nesco SnackMaster. This refreshing tea blend is also perfect for gift giving.

Prep time: 10 minutes | Cook time: 12 hours | Servings: 24

Ingredients:

1 bunch fresh peppermint

6 strawberries, minced

2 oz. black tea

Instructions:

1. Wash and dry your fresh mint and remove the leaves from the stems.

2. Place a Clean-A-Screen on one of the racks of your Nesco SnackMaster. Place the minced strawberry on the screen. Place the mint leaves on the other racks and set your SnackMaster to 125F. Dehydrate for 12 hours.

3. When mint and strawberries are completely dried, remove them from the racks and place in a medium bowl. Mix well and add the black tea leaves. Divide the mixture into jars or zip-lock bags until ready to use.

4. To brew a cup of tea, boil 8 ounces of water and use one teaspoon of tea blend per cup. Pour the boiling water over the tea or use an infuser. Steep for five minutes and enjoy.

Nutritional Info: Calories: 2, Sodium: 1 mg, Dietary Fiber: 0.2 g, Fat: 0 g, Carbs: 0.4 g, Protein: 0.1 g.

Fruit and Herb Tea

This bright herbal tea is brimming with zesty flavors. Perfect when you want a soothing cup of tea, but don't want caffeine keeping you up all night.

Prep time: 20 minutes | Cook time: 6 hours | Servings: 12

Ingredients:

Zest of 2 lemons, minced

Zest of 2 oranges, minced

1 cup peppermint leaves

1 cup dried cranberries

1 tablespoon fresh ginger, minced

Instructions:

1. In a medium bowl, combine the lemon zest, orange zest, mint leaves, cranberries, and ginger. Mix well.

2. Place Clean-A-Screens on the racks of your Nesco SnackMaster and place the mixture evenly on the screens. Set your SnackMaster to 150F and dehydrate for 6 hours.

3. When everything is completely dried, remove the contents of the dehydrator and place in a bowl. Mix well and divide into jars or zip-lock bags until ready to use.

4. To brew a cup of tea, boil 8 ounces of water and use one teaspoon of tea blend per cup. Pour the boiling water over the tea or use an infuser. Steep for five minutes and enjoy.

Nutritional Info: Calories: 27, Sodium: 3 mg, Dietary Fiber: 2.2 g, Fat: 0.2 g, Carbs: 6.1 g, Protein: 0.7 g.

Lemon Chamomile Tea

This classic herbal tea is made even more relaxing and delicious with fresh ingredients dehydrated to perfection in your Nesco SnackMaster.

Prep time: 15 minutes | Cook time: 6 hours | Servings: 12

Ingredients:

1 bunch fresh peppermint

1/2 cup lavender flowers

1/2 cup Chamomile flowers

Zest from 4 lemons, chopped

2 tablespoons fresh ginger, chopped

Instructions:

1. Wash peppermint and remove the leaves from the stems. Place the mint, lavender, Chamomile, lemon zest, and ginger evenly on the racks of your Nesco SnackMaster.

2. Set your SnackMaster to 125F and dehydrate for six hours. When everything is completely dried, pour the contents of the dehydrator into a large bowl. Mix well and divide into jars or zip-lock bags.

3. To brew a cup of tea, boil 8 ounces of water and use one teaspoon of tea blend per cup. Pour the boiling water over the tea or use an infuser. Steep for five minutes and enjoy.

Nutritional Info: Calories: 30, Sodium: 62 mg, Dietary Fiber: 1.1 g, Fat: 2.9 g, Carbs: 3.9 g, Protein: 0.5 g.

Orange Spice Tea

This robust black tea blend is a great way to start your day with a variety of flavors and a kick of caffeine to get you going on busy mornings.

Prep time: 15 minutes | Cook time: 6 hours | Servings: 24

Ingredients:

Zest of 2 oranges

Zest of 2 lemons

1 cup Darjeeling tea

2 cinnamon sticks, roughly chopped

1/4 cup cardamom pods, roughly chopped

Instructions:

1. Peel the zest from the oranges and lemons. It's ok if they are large pieces. Place the zest on a rack in your Nesco SnackMaster and set to 125F. Dehydrate for 6 hours or until the zest is completely dried.

2. Remove the zest from the rack and roughly chop into small pieces. In a medium bowl, combine the zest, tea leaves, cinnamon, and cardamom. Mix well and divide into jars or zip-lock bags.

3. To brew a cup of tea, boil 8 ounces of water and use one teaspoon of tea blend per cup. Pour the boiling water over the tea or use an infuser. Steep for five minutes and enjoy.

Nutritional Info: Calories: 13, Sodium: 1 mg, Dietary Fiber: 0.9 g, Fat: 0.1 g, Carbs: 3.2 g, Protein: 0.3 g.

Vanilla Cornflower Tea

This earthy tea blend is great any time of day. The addition of cornflower adds a floral hint that perfectly complements the elegant flavor of traditional Earl Grey tea.

Prep time: 10 minutes | Cook time: 6 hours | Servings: 12

Ingredients:

1/2 cup cornflowers

1 cup Earl Grey tea

1 vanilla bean

Instructions:

1. Place the cornflowers on one rack of your Nesco SnackMaster and place the vanilla bean on another rack. Set your SnackMaster to 125F. and dehydrate for 6 hours.

2. Remove the flowers and place them in a bowl. Roughly chop the vanilla bean and add it to the bowl with the flowers. Add the Earl Grey tea and mix well. Divide evenly among jars or zipper lock bags.

3. To brew a cup of tea, boil 8 ounces of water and use one teaspoon of tea blend per cup. Pour the boiling water over the tea or use an infuser. Steep for five minutes and enjoy.

Nutritional Info: Calories: 13, Sodium: 8 mg, Dietary Fiber: 0.1 g, Fat: 0 g, Carbs: 2.3 g, Protein: 0.5 g.

Digestive Tea

This delicious tea is perfect for enjoying any time, but the combination of medicinal herbs and flowers also has the amazing ability sooth an upset stomach.

Prep time: 10 minutes | Cook time: 6 hours | Servings: 12

Ingredients:

1/2 cup lemongrass, roughly chopped

1/4 cup fresh ginger, roughly chopped

1/4 cup licorice root, roughly chopped

Instructions:

1. Place a Clean-A-Screen on one of the racks of your Nesco SnackMaster. Place the lemongrass, ginger, and licorice root on the screen and spread out so it is no more than 1/4 inch thick.

2. Set your SnackMaster to 150F. and dehydrate for 6 hours.

3. When everything is completely dried, remove from the screen and place in a medium bowl. Stir well to combine and divide into jars or zip-lock bags to store.

4. To brew a cup of tea, boil 8 ounces of water and use one teaspoon of tea blend per cup. Pour the boiling water over the tea or use an infuser. Steep for five minutes and enjoy.

Nutritional Info: Calories: 9, Sodium: 1 mg, Dietary Fiber: 0.2 g, Fat: 0.1 g, Carbs: 2 g, Protein: 0.2 g.

Rosemary Mint Tea

The combination of fragrant rosemary with delicate peppermint creates a perfectly balanced tea blend which can be enjoyed any time.

Prep time: 10 minutes | Cook time: 6 hours | Servings: 12

Ingredients:

6 sprigs fresh rosemary   *Green or black tea*
2 bunches fresh mint

Instructions:

1. Wash the herbs and remove the leaves from the mint stems. Do not remove the rosemary leaves from the stems.

2. Place the mint leaves and rosemary sprigs on the racks of your Nesco SnackMaster, set for 125F. and dehydrate for 6 hours.

3. When the herbs are completely dried, remove from the racks and place in a medium bowl. Add the tea leaves and stir well. Divide among jars or zip-lock bags to store.

4. To brew a cup of tea, boil 8 ounces of water and use one teaspoon of tea blend per cup. Pour the boiling water over the tea or use an infuser. Steep for five minutes and enjoy.

Nutritional Info: Calories: 14, Sodium: 7 mg, Dietary Fiber: 2 g, Fat: 0.4 g, Carbs: 2.7 g, Protein: 0.7 g.

Lemon Sage Tea

The combination of bright citrus and floral notes makes for a perfectly flavored cup of tea which is great on a summer day. Try this tea hot or iced for delicious results.

Prep time: 15 minutes | Cook time: 6 hours | Servings: 12

Ingredients:

1 cup Chamomile flowers

Peel from 1 lemon

1/2 cup peppermint leaves

1/2 cup fresh sage

1/2 cup black or green tea

Instructions:

1. Remove the peel from one lemon and chop into small pieces. Place the lemon peel, Chamomile flowers, peppermint leaves, and sage on the racks of your Nesco SnackMaster.

2. Set your SnackMaster for 125F. and dehydrate for 6 hours. Remove the contents of the racks and place in a large bowl. Add the tea leaves and stir well to combine. Divide among jars or zip-lock bags to store.

3. To brew a cup of tea, boil 8 ounces of water and use one teaspoon of tea blend per cup. Pour the boiling water over the tea or use an infuser. Steep for five minutes and enjoy.

Nutritional Info: Calories: 6, Sodium: 1 mg, Dietary Fiber: 0.9 g, Fat: 0.2 g, Carbs: 1.3 g, Protein: 0.3 g.

Apple Mint Tea

Apple and mint combine for tea that is herbal and just a little sweet thanks to the natural flavors of fresh apples. This tea works perfectly as iced tea on a hot summer day.

Prep time: 15 minutes | Cook time: 12 hours | Servings: 12

Ingredients:

1 red delicious apple

1 bunch fresh mint

1 cup black or green tea

Instructions:

1. Slice apples into thin 1/8-inch slices. Wash the mint and remove the leaves from the stems.

2. Place the apple slices and mint leaves on the racks of your Nesco SnackMaster. Set your SnackMaster to 135F. and dehydrate for 12 hours. When the apple slices are completely dry, remove from the SnackMaster and chop the apples into small pieces.

3. In a medium bowl, combine the apple, mint, and tea leaves. Mix well and store in jars or zip-lock bags.

4. To brew a cup of tea, boil 8 ounces of water and use one teaspoon of tea blend per cup. Pour the boiling water over the tea or use an infuser. Steep for five minutes and enjoy.

Nutritional Info: Calories: 5, Sodium: 2 mg, Dietary Fiber: 0.8 g, Fat: 0.1 g, Carbs: 3 g, Protein: 0.2 g.

Hibiscus Tea

This exotic blend is a bit sweet and a bit floral and is sure to be a hit at tea parties or as a soothing way to start your day.

Prep time: 5 minutes | Cook time: 6 hours | Servings: 6

Ingredients:

1/4 cup hibiscus flowers

1/4 cup cranberries

1/2 cup green tea

Instructions:

1. Place a Clean-A-Screen on a rack in your SnackMaster. Place the hibiscus flowers and cranberries on the screen and set the SnackMaster to 135F. Dehydrate for 6 hours or until the cranberries are almost completely dried.

2. Remove the contents of the SnackMaster and place in a medium bowl. Add the green tea and mix well. Store in jars or zip-lock bags.

3. To brew a cup of tea, boil 8 ounces of water and use one teaspoon of tea blend per cup. Pour the boiling water over the tea or use an infuser. Steep for five minutes and enjoy.

Nutritional Info: Calories: 3, Sodium: 0 mg, Dietary Fiber: 0.2 g, Fat: 0 g, Carbs: 0.4 g, Protein: 0 g.

10

BREAKFAST

Buckwheat Granola

This wholesome granola is perfect for a healthy breakfast or a filling midday snack. Making your own granola also allows you to control the ingredients and limit added sugar.

Prep time: 20 minutes | Cook time: 12 hours | Servings: 6

Ingredients:

1 cup almonds, sliced

1/2 cup pecans, chopped

1/4 cup sunflower seeds

1/4 cup pumpkin seeds

1 cup apple sauce

1/4 cup flax seeds

1/2 cup dried cranberries

1 tablespoon ground cinnamon

1 tablespoon brown sugar

1/4 cup sesame seeds

Instructions:

1.   In a large bowl, combine all ingredients and mix well.

2.   Place Clean-A-Screens on the rack of your Nesco SnackMaster. Spread the mixture evenly on the screens and set your SnackMaster to 115F.

3.   Dehydrate for 12 hours or until completely dried. Serve with yogurt or milk.

Nutritional Info: Calories: 296, Sodium: 4 mg, Dietary Fiber: 6.7 g, Fat: 24.4 g, Carbs: 14.4 g, Protein: 8.4 g.

Yogurt

Yogurt is a great, healthy way to start the day and thanks to your Nesco SnackMaster, you can make delicious, flavorful yogurt any time.

Prep time: 5 minutes | Cook time: 15 hours | Servings: 20

Ingredients:

1-gallon whole milk   *2 cups plain yogurt*

Instructions:

1. In a large pot, heat the milk to 140F.

2. Remove from heat and allow the milk to cool to 118F.

3. Add the yogurt and stir well. Pour the milk into small glass jars which will fit inside your SnackMaster.

4. Set your SnackMaster to 110F and cook for at least 12 hours for mild yogurt, or 15 hours for more tart yogurt. The longer you cook the yogurt to stronger and thicker the yogurt will become.

5. Remove the jars from the SnackMaster and chill before eating.

Nutritional Info: Calories: 133, Sodium: 94 mg, Dietary Fiber: 0 g, Fat: 6.5 g, Carbs: 10.4 g, Protein: 7.6 g.

Homemade Powdered Eggs

Perfect for camping, these homemade dried eggs just require water and can be stored for months without being refrigerated.

Prep time: 10 minutes | Cook time: 18 hours | Servings: 12

Ingredients:

12 eggs

2 tablespoons vegetable oil

Instructions:

1. In a large bowl, beat the eggs thoroughly.

2. In a large skillet, over medium high heat, add the oil. When the oil begins shimmering, add the eggs and scramble. Remove from heat and allow to cool.

3. Place Clean-A-Screens on the racks of your SnackMaster and spread the scrambled eggs evenly on the racks.

4. Set your SnackMaster to 145F and dehydrate for 18 hours.

5. When eggs are completely dried, remove from the SnackMaster and place in a food processor. Pulse for a few seconds until the eggs have a uniform texture. Store in an airtight container.

Nutritional Info: Calories: 83, Sodium: 62 mg, Dietary Fiber: 0 g, Fat: 6.6 g, Carbs: 0.3 g, Protein: 5.5 g.

Walnut Cinnamon Cereal

This richly flavored cereal is healthy and delicious. By using your Nesco SnackMaster to make your own cereal, you can save time and avoid added fat and sugar.

Prep time: 10 minutes | Cook time: 10 hours | Servings: 4

Ingredients:

---

4 cups walnuts

5 tablespoons maple syrup

3 tablespoons dried coconut

1/2 cup fresh cranberries

1/2 teaspoon vanilla

1 teaspoon ground cinnamon

1 teaspoon ground nutmeg

4 bananas

Instructions:

---

1. In a food processor, combine the maple syrup, coconut, cranberries, vanilla, cinnamon, nutmeg, and bananas. Pulse until smooth.

2. In a large bowl, combine the mixture with the walnuts and stir well.

3. Place Clean-A-Screens on the racks of your Nesco SnackMaster and spread the walnut mixture, evenly, on the screens. Set your SnackMaster to 110F and dehydrate for two hours.

4. Mix the contents of the dehydrator and dehydrate an additional 8 hours. Remove the cereal from the SnackMaster and crush into small pieces. Serve with milk or yogurt.

Nutritional Info: Calories: 969, Sodium: 7 mg, Dietary Fiber: 12.8 g, Fat: 75.7 g, Carbs: 58.7 g, Protein: 31.6 g.

Maple Granola

This simple maple flavored granola is easy to make and is sure to delight the entire family. Your Nesco SnackMaster ensure your granola is dehydrated to the perfect consistency.

Prep time: 24 hours | Cook time: 24 hours | Servings: 8

Ingredients:

1 cup coconut	1 1/2 cup maple syrup
2 cups raw almonds	1/4 cup melted coconut oil
2 cups walnuts	2 tablespoons vanilla
1 cup pecans	2 tablespoons cinnamon
1 cup cashews	2 tablespoons salt

Instructions:

1. In a large bowl, combine nuts and cover with water. Add salt, stir and allow to sit for 24 hours.

2. Drain the nuts and dry the nuts with paper towels. Place the nuts in a food processor and pulse until the nuts are broken down into small pieces.

3. Transfer nut mixture to a large bowl and stir in the maple syrup, coconut oil, cinnamon, and vanilla. Stir well.

4. Place Clean-A-Screens on the racks of your SnackMaster and evenly spread the nut mixture. Set your SnackMaster to 125F and dehydrate for 24 hours.

5. Remove granola from the screens and allow to cool before storing.

Nutritional Info: Calories: 792, Sodium: 809 mg, Dietary Fiber: 9.1 g, Fat: 58.6 g, Carbs: 59 g, Protein: 17.3 g.

Breakfast Bars

These healthy and delicious granola bars are a great way to start the day, and they also make a perfect snack for hiking and camping.

Prep time: 12 hours | Cook time: 12 hours | Servings: 8

Ingredients:

4 cups oats

2 tablespoons buttermilk

2 cups dried coconut

1 cup almonds, chopped

1 cup walnuts, chopped

1 cup raisins or dried cranberries

1/2 cup melted coconut oil

3 tablespoon maple syrup

Instructions:

1. Place the oats in a large bowl and cover with water. Add the buttermilk and allow to soak for 12 hours.

2. Drain the oats and place in a large bowl. Stir in the coconut, almonds, walnuts, cranberries, coconut oil, and maple syrup. Mix well.

3. Place Clean-A-Screens on the racks of your Nesco SnackMaster. Use a large spoon to make the mixture into balls. Place the balls on the screens and flatten them a bit with the back of the spoon.

4. Set your SnackMaster to 125F and dehydrate for 12 hours, flipping the bars halfway through.

Nutritional Info: Calories: 516, Sodium: 67 mg, Dietary Fiber: 9.2 g, Fat: 30.3 g, Carbs: 54.3 g, Protein: 13 g.

Vanilla Wheat Cereal

This crispy cereal is healthy and delicious thanks to rich vanilla extract and earthy spices. Once you've made this cereal, you may never buy cereal again.

Prep time: 12 hours | Cook time: 12 hours | Servings: 6

Ingredients:

----

6 cups buckwheat

1 1/2 tablespoons vanilla extract

2 cups applesauce

1 tablespoon cinnamon

1 teaspoon allspice

2 teaspoons salt

Instructions:

----

1. In a large bowl, soak the buckwheat for 12 hours and drain.

2. In a food processor, add the buckwheat, vanilla, applesauce, cinnamon, allspice, and salt. Pulse until the mixture forms a loose paste.

3. Place Clean-A-Screens on the racks of your SnackMaster and spread the mixture evenly on the screens.

4. Set your SnackMaster to 115F and dehydrate for 12 hours or until completely dried. Remove the cereal from the racks and break into small pieces. Store in an air tight container.

Nutritional Info: Calories: 332, Sodium: 786 mg, Dietary Fiber: 10.1 g, Fat: 2.3 g, Carbs: 72.2 g, Protein: 9.8 g.

Coconut Pancakes

These unique pancakes are packed with flavor, easy to make, and completely vegan. Perfect for breakfast or dessert, these pancakes are sure to be a hit.

Prep time: 15 minutes | Cook time: 18 hours | Servings: 5

Ingredients:

1 cup dried cranberries

4 cups banana, chopped

1 cup water

1/2 cup coconut flesh

1/2 teaspoon vanilla extract

1/2 cup fresh blueberries

Instructions:

1. Place Clean-A-Screens on the racks of your Nesco SnackMaster. Spread the chopped bananas on the racks in 3 to 4-inch rounds. Set your SnackMaster to 115F and dehydrate for 18 hours.

2. In a small bowl, combine the water, cranberries, vanilla, and coconut. Mix well.

3. Remove the banana pancakes from the screens and top with coconut cream and blueberries to serve.

Nutritional Info: Calories: 157, Sodium: 4 mg, Dietary Fiber: 5 g, Fat: 3.1 g, Carbs: 32.8 g, Protein: 1.7 g.

Green Pepper Omelet

This quick and easy omelet uses green peppers partially dried in your Nesco SnackMaster. The partial dehydration process concentrates the flavor while keeping the nutrients intact.

Prep time: 10 minutes | Cook time: 6 hours | Servings: 2

Ingredients:

6 eggs

2 green peppers

2 tablespoons butter

Salt and black pepper

Instructions:

1. Slice the green pepper into thin strips.

2. Set your Nesco SnackMaster to 125F and lay the green pepper strips on the racks. Dehydrate for 6 hours.

3. Remove the green peppers from the racks. They will not be completely dried.

4. In a large bowl, beat the eggs and heat a medium skillet over medium heat.

5. Add 1 tablespoon of butter to the pan and when melted, add half of the eggs. Place strips of green pepper on the eggs, and flip to close the omelet. Season with salt and pepper before serving.

6. Repeat step five to make an additional omelet.

Nutritional Info: Calories: 314, Sodium: 270 mg, Dietary Fiber: 2 g, Fat: 24.8 g, Carbs: 6.6 g, Protein: 17.8 g.

Cranberry Muffins

This delicious muffin recipe uses cranberries dried to perfection in your Nesco SnackMaster. We think you'll find they are the most flavorful muffins you've ever had.

Prep time: 20 minutes | Cook time: 9 hours | Servings: 12

Ingredients:

2 cups fresh cranberries

2 cups flour

2/3 cups sugar

2 teaspoons baking powder

1/2 teaspoon salt

2/3 cups whole milk

1/4 cup butter, melted

1 egg, beaten

1/2 teaspoon vanilla extract

Instructions:

1. Heat a large pot of water to boiling. Add the cranberries and boil for two minutes. Drain the cranberries and place them on the rack of your Nesco SnackMaster. Set your dehydrator to 135F and dehydrate for 8 hours.

2. When cranberries are finished dehydrating, combine the flour, sugar, baking powder, and salt in a large bowl. Stir in the cranberries, milk, butter, egg, and mix well.

3. Heat your oven to 400F. Pour the muffin batter into 12 muffin tins and bake for 18 to 20 minutes. Remove muffins from the oven and allow them to sit in the pan for 5 minutes before transferring them to a wire rack to cool.

Nutritional Info: Calories: 176, Sodium: 136 mg, Dietary Fiber: 1.3 g, Fat: 4.8 g, Carbs: 29.7 g, Protein: 3.1 g.

11

SOUP and STEW

Vegetable Soup

This amazing vegetable soup is designed to be made ahead and rehydrated with a moment's notice. Perfect for camping and hiking, but also ideal for a quick weeknight dinner when you don't feel like cooking but want a home cooked meal.

Prep time: 20 minutes | Cook time: 6 hours | Servings: 10

Ingredients:

1 large potato, peeled and sliced

1/2 yellow onion, sliced

1/2 cup tomato, chopped

1 zucchini, sliced

2 large carrots, peeled and sliced

1/4 cup vegetable bouillon powder

Instructions:

1. Arrange the sliced vegetables on the racks of your Nesco SnackMaster. Set your dehydrator to 125F and dehydrate for 6 hours.

2. When everything is completely dried, remove from the racks and layer in a large mason jar until ready to use.

3. To make the soup. Combine the contents of the jar with 12 cups of water in a large pot. Cook until vegetables are tender.

Nutritional Info: Calories: 53, Sodium: 440 mg, Dietary Fiber: 1.6 g, Fat: 0.6 g, Carbs: 10.9 g, Protein: 1.7 g.

Tomato Bean Soup

This rich and hearty soup is perfect for a cold winter day. Your Nesco SnackMaster ensures that all of the ingredients are dehydrated to perfection, so this soup mix will last as long as possible.

Prep time: 15 minutes | Cook time: 10 hours | Servings: 6

Ingredients:

1 cup dehydrated Mirepoix (see recipe 17)

1/2 cup green beans, chopped

1 cup cannellini beans

3 tomatoes, chopped

1 clove garlic, minced

2 tablespoons chicken bouillon powder

1 teaspoon dried thyme

1 teaspoon dried rosemary

1 tablespoon salt

Instructions:

1. Place the green beans and tomatoes on the racks of your SnackMaster and set to 125F. Dehydrate for 10 hours.

2. Remove from the racks and layer in a jar in the following order from the bottom up: Mirepoix, rosemary, thyme, bouillon powder, green beans, cannellini beans, tomatoes, garlic, and salt. Store in a cool dark place until ready to use.

3. To prepare soup, combine contents of jar with 10 cups water. Bring to a boil and reduce to a simmer until all of the ingredients are tender.

Nutritional Info: Calories: 118, Sodium: 203 mg, Dietary Fiber: 8.9 g, Fat: 0.4 g, Carbs: 21.9 g, Protein: 8 g.

Black Bean Soup

This delicious protein rich soup is perfect for hiking or camping trips. Simply dehydrate all of the ingredients in your Nesco SnackMaster and rehydrate over an open fire to serve.

Prep time: 15 minutes | Cook time: 12 hours | Servings: 6

Ingredients:

2 cups black beans

1 large tomato, diced

2 cloves garlic, finely chopped

1 yellow onion, finely chopped

1 red bell pepper, sliced

1/2 cup cilantro leaves

1 teaspoon chili powder

1 teaspoon ground cumin

1 teaspoon red pepper flakes

1 tablespoon salt

Instructions:

1. Place the bean, tomato, garlic, onion, red pepper, and cilantro on the racks of your Nesco SnackMaster. Set to 125F. and dehydrate for 12 hours.

2. Remove the vegetables from the racks and place in a blender with the chili powder, cumin, red pepper flakes, and salt. Blend until a fine powder form. Store the soup mix in jars or zip-lock bags.

3. To make soup, use three tablespoons of soup mix per cup of boiling water. Stir well and enjoy.

Nutritional Info: Calories: 245, Sodium: 1174 mg, Dietary Fiber: 11.2 g, Fat: 1.3 g, Carbs: 45.7 g, Protein: 14.9 g.

Dehydrated Chili

Making a pot of chili can be time consuming, but this easy recipe allows you to have delicious chili ready to make at a moment's notice.

Prep time: 15 minutes | Cook time: 10 hours | Servings: 6

Ingredients:

2 russet potatoes, cubed

1/2 lb. ground beef

1/4 cup kidney beans

1 tomato, diced

1 yellow onion, chopped

4 tablespoons tomato paste

4 tablespoons home dehydrated chili powder (see recipe: 19)

Instructions:

1. Place Clean-A-Screens on one rack of your Nesco SnackMaster. Use this rack for the tomato paste. On other racks arrange the potatoes, beef, beans, tomato, and onion. Set your dehydrator for 125F. and dehydrate for 10 hours.

2. When everything is completely dehydrated, remove from racks and place in a large mason jar or zip-lock bag with the chili powder.

3. To make chili, combine the contents of the jar with 4 cups boiling water. Stir well and enjoy.

Nutritional Info: Calories: 163, Sodium: 42 mg, Dietary Fiber: 3.8 g, Fat: 2.6 g, Carbs: 20 g, Protein: 15.1 g.

Chicken Bouillon Powder

Instead of buying commercially made chicken bouillon which can be packed with artificial ingredients, use your Nesco SnackMaster to create all-natural chicken bouillon that can be used in a wide variety of dishes.

Prep time: 2 hours | Cook time: 24 hours | Servings: 20

Ingredients:

1 whole chicken, cut into pieces

1 cup dehydrated Mirepoix (see recipe: 17)

Instructions:

1. Heat a large pot of water and add the chicken pieces, cooking covered for 1 1/2 hours. Remove the chicken pieces from the broth and continue cooking uncovered until the broth has reduced to about 2 cups.

2. Place Clean-A-Screens on the racks of your SnackMaster. Set to 150F. and dehydrate for 24 hours or until the broth has become a solid, dry wafer.

3. Remove dried broth from racks and combine with the dried Mirepoix in a blender. Blend until a fine powder form. Store in jars or zip-lock bags until ready to use.

4. To rehydrate broth, combine 1 tablespoon of broth powder with 1 cup boiling water.

Nutritional Info: Calories: 55, Sodium: 20 mg, Dietary Fiber: 0.1 g, Fat: 3.2 g, Carbs: 0.3 g, Protein: 5.8 g.

Minestrone

This classic Italian soup is great any time of year. This easy dehydrated soup mix guarantees your minestrone is always fresh tasting and nutritious.

Prep time: 15 minutes | Cook time: 12 hours | Servings: 6

Ingredients:

6 tablespoons chicken bouillon powder (see recipe: 65)

1/2 yellow onion, finely chopped

2 cloves garlic, finely minced

4 tablespoons tomato powder (see recipe: 16)

1 12 oz. can Cannellini beans

1 cup macaroni

1 tablespoon black pepper

Instructions:

1. Place a Clean-A-Screen on one rack of your Nesco SnackMaster. On this rack place the minced garlic. On the other racks, arrange the onions and beans. Set your dehydrator for 125F. and dehydrate for 12 hours.

2. Remove the vegetables from the racks and combine with the chicken bouillon, tomato powder, macaroni, and pepper. Store in a jar or zip-lock bag until ready to use.

3. To make soup, combine the contents of the jar with 6 cups boiling water and simmer until the pasta and beans are soft.

Nutritional Info: Calories: 55, Sodium: 20 mg, Dietary Fiber: 0.1 g, Fat: 3.2 g, Carbs: 0.3 g, Protein: 5.8 g.

Coconut Curry Soup

This creamy Thai inspired soup is easy to make and is packed with a variety of complex flavors that are sure to delight your family or guests.

Prep time: 10 minutes | Cook time: 24 hours | Servings: 4

Ingredients:

1 can coconut milk

2 tablespoons chicken bouillon powder (see recipe: 65)

2 teaspoons curry powder

dried rice noodles

1 zucchini, chopped

1 red bell pepper, chopped

Instructions:

1. Place coconut milk in containers small enough to fit inside your Nesco SnackMaster. Place the zucchini and peppers on separate racks. Set to 135F and dehydrate for 24 hours or until dried. Remove the zucchini and peppers from the dehydrator and set aside. Place the dehydrated coconut milk in a blender with the chicken bouillon and curry powder and blend until a fine powder form.

2. Combine the powder with the dried vegetables and noodles and store in a large zip-lock bag.

3. To make soup, combine the contents of the bag with 3 cups boiling water. Simmer until noodles and vegetables are soft.

Nutritional Info: Calories: 159, Sodium: 58 mg, Dietary Fiber: 2.6 g, Fat: 14.6 g, Carbs: 7.9 g, Protein: 2.4 g.

Dehydrated Bone Broth

Bone broth has gained popularity in recent years because it is an excellent source of protein and collagen which has many nutritional properties. Making a batch of bone broth takes time, but your Nesco SnackMaster allows you to dehydrate bone broth to use anytime.

Prep time: 5 minutes | Cook time: 24 hours | Servings: 20

Ingredients:

5 lbs. beef shin bones

10 cups water

3 tablespoons salt

Instructions:

1. In a large stock pot combine beef bones, water and salt. Boil until a strong broth develops. Remove the bones and discard.

2. Continue cooking broth until it resembles thick gravy. Remove from heat.

3. Place Clean-A-Screens on the racks of your Nesco SnackMaster and spread the gravy evenly on the screens. Set your dehydrator to 150F. and dehydrate until solid. Remove from the screens and cut into one-inch chunks.

Nutritional Info: Calories: 143, Sodium: 150 mg, Dietary Fiber: 0.6 g, Fat: 7 g, Carbs: 0.3 g, Protein: 19.4 g.

Split Pea Soup

Use your Nesco SnackMaster to dehydrate pea soup so you always have some on hand. You will never want to buy pre-made soup again after you've tasted this delicious creamy soup.

Prep time: 2 hours | Cook time: 8 hours | Servings: 6

Ingredients:

2 cups split peas

2 cups carrots, chopped

1 clove garlic, minced

1 cup onion, chopped

1 cup celery, chopped

8 cups chicken broth

1 tablespoon olive oil

Instructions:

1. Heat the olive oil in a large pot over medium heat, and add the onion, garlic, carrot, and celery. Cook until the vegetables are soft.

2. Add the chicken broth and peas and bring to a boil. Reduce to a simmer and cook for 2 hours. Remove from heat and puree with a blender.

3. Place Clean-A-Screens on the racks of your Nesco SnackMaster and spread the pea soup in an even layer. Set your dehydrator for 125F and cook for 8 hours. When soup is completely dried, remove from the SnackMaster and place in a blender. Blend until a fine powder form. Store in jars or zip-lock bags.

Nutritional Info: Calories: 321, Sodium: 1067 mg, Dietary Fiber: 18.3 g, Fat: 5 g, Carbs: 46.9 g, Protein: 23.2 g.

Beef and Vegetable Soup

This classic beef and vegetable soup is easy to make and incredibly satisfying. Using your Nesco SnackMaster to dehydrate means you always have fresh soup ready to eat.

Prep time: 10 minutes | Cook time: 12 hours | Servings: 6

Ingredients:

1 lb. beef chuck roast, cut into chunks

2 carrots, chopped

1/2 cup green beans, chopped

1 russet potato, cubed

1/2 cup peas

1/2 cup celery

1 yellow onion, chopped

1 tablespoon salt

1 teaspoon black pepper

Instructions:

1. Place the beef on the racks of your dehydrator and set to 165F. Dehydrate for 6 hours or until completely dried. Remove from dehydrator.

2. Place carrots, green beans, potatoes, peas, celery, and onion on the racks of the SnackMaster and set to 135F. Dehydrate for 6 hours or until completely dried.

3. In a large zip-lock bag, combine the beef, vegetables, salt, and pepper. Store until ready to use.

4. To make soup, combine the contents of the bag with 3 cups boiling water. Simmer until beef is cooked through and vegetables are tender.

Nutritional Info: Calories: 322, Sodium: 234 mg, Dietary Fiber: 2.5 g, Fat: 21.1 g, Carbs: 10.9 g, Protein: 21.7 g.

12

MAIN COURSES

Roast Chicken with Dried Citrus

Citrus fruit is the perfect complement to roast chicken, and the citrus you make in your Nesco SnackMaster is guaranteed to be bursting with concentrated flavor.

Prep time: 20 minutes | Cook time: 2 1/2 hours | Servings: 6

Ingredients:

1 whole chicken

1 orange, sliced into rounds and dehydrated

1 lemon, sliced into rounds and dehydrated

1 sprig fresh thyme

1 sprig fresh rosemary

4 tablespoons butter

Salt and black pepper

Instructions:

1. Rinse and dry the chicken and place in a roasting pan. Set your oven to 375F.

2. Place the herbs, 2 tablespoons of butter, and three slices each of lemon and orange in the cavity of the chicken.

3. Place the remaining butter under the skin on the breasts of the chicken. Lay the additional citrus slices on the skin of the chicken and place in the oven for 2 hours.

4. Use and instant read thermometer to make sure the chicken is 165F. If not, cook an additional 30 minutes.

Nutritional Info: Calories: 230, Sodium: 116 mg, Dietary Fiber: 1.6 g, Fat: 17.2 g, Carbs: 5.7 g, Protein: 14.6 g.

Chicken with Blackberries

This creative recipe for chicken breasts is easy to make and uses blackberries dehydrated in your Nesco SnackMaster. You can try this recipe with a variety of berries you've dehydrated at home.

Prep time: 20 minutes | Cook time: 20 minutes | Servings: 6

Ingredients:

6 chicken breasts, trimmed

3/4 cups dehydrated blackberries

1/2 cup chicken stock

2 tablespoons brown sugar

2 cloves garlic, minced

1 teaspoon paprika

1/2 teaspoon ground cumin

2 teaspoons dried thyme

1 tablespoon olive oil

1 teaspoon salt

1/2 teaspoon black pepper

2 teaspoons cornstarch

Instructions:

1. In a large bowl, combine 1/4 cup blackberries, 1/4 cup chicken stock, oil, garlic, paprika, and cumin. Mix well into a paste.

2. Preheat oven to 375F and place the chicken breasts in a baking dish and coat with blackberry paste. Season with thyme, salt, and pepper. Bake for 20 minutes or until an instant read thermometer reads 165F.

3. Remove chicken from the baking dish and pour pan juices into a small saucepan with the remaining chicken stock, blackberries, and cornstarch over medium heat. Whisk until thickened.

Nutritional Info: Calories: 93, Sodium: 663 mg, Dietary Fiber: 1.3 g, Fat: 3.1 g, Carbs: 6.5 g, Protein: 10.5 g.

Asian Beef with Dehydrated Vegetables

This Asian inspired dish combines tender strips of beef with vegetables dehydrated and preserved using your Nesco SnackMaster. Because your dehydrated veggies are always on hand, this dish is easy to make after a busy day.

Prep time: 20 minutes | Cook time: 20 minutes | Servings: 4

Ingredients:

1 lb. sirloin steak, sliced into strips

2 tablespoons soy sauce

2 tablespoons mirin

2 tablespoons vegetable oil

1/2 cup dehydrated broccoli

1/2 cup dehydrated green pepper

1/2 cup dehydrated zucchini

2 cloves garlic, minced

1/2 cup chicken broth

2 teaspoons cornstarch

Instructions:

1. In a large bowl, combine the beef, soy sauce, mirin, and cornstarch. Stir well.

2. In a large skillet over medium-high heat, add half of the oil. When oil is shimmering, add the dehydrated vegetables and chicken broth and garlic. Cook for several minutes or until the vegetables are rehydrated.

3. Pour contents of pan into a large bowl and add the rest of the oil to the pan. Increase to high heat and add the beef, cooking until browned on the outside. Add the vegetable mix back to the pan and stir well before serving.

Nutritional Info: Calories: 308, Sodium: 690 mg, Dietary Fiber: 0.8 g, Fat: 14.1 g, Carbs: 7.7 g, Protein: 36.2 g.

Meaty Bolognese

This convenient take on a traditional Bolognese sauce is great because you can prepare many of the ingredients ahead of time and rehydrate when you're ready to eat.

Prep time: 15 minutes | Cook time: 45 minutes | Servings: 6

Ingredients:

1 cup dehydrated tomato slices

1/4 cup dehydrated onion

1/4 cup dehydrated celery

1/4 cup dehydrated carrot

2 cloves garlic, minced

2 cups water

2 cups chicken broth

1/2 lb. ground beef

1/2 lb. ground pork

1 teaspoon salt

1 teaspoon black pepper

1 teaspoon dehydrated oregano

Pasta of your choice

Instructions:

1. In a large bowl, crush the tomatoes, and add the onion, celery, carrot, garlic, and water. Allow the vegetables to rehydrate.

2. In a large skillet over medium heat, brown the beef and pork, adding the salt, pepper, and oregano as it cooks. Add the vegetable mixture and broth, and simmer for 30 minutes. When the sauce is nearly finished, heat a pot of salted water and cook pasta. Serve the sauce over pasta.

Nutritional Info: Calories: 173, Sodium: 759 mg, Dietary Fiber: 1 g, Fat: 5.7 g, Carbs: 5.5 g, Protein: 23.7 g.

Mushroom Crusted Beef Tenderloin

Beef tenderloin and mushrooms have always partnered well, and this recipe allows you to use fragrant dehydrated mushrooms from your Nesco SnackMaster as a delicate crust for a whole tenderloin.

Prep time: 20 minutes | Cook time: 40 minutes | Servings: 8

Ingredients:

4 lbs. beef tenderloin

1/2 cup dehydrated porcini mushrooms

4 tablespoons olive oil

Salt and black pepper

Instructions:

1. Season the beef with salt and pepper and set your oven to 350F. Place the beef on a rack in a roasting pan and place in the oven for 10 minutes.

2. While the beef is cooking, place the dehydrated mushrooms in a blender and blend into a powder.

3. Remove the beef from the oven and rub on all sides with the mushroom powder. Place back in the oven for approximately 30 to 40 minutes, or until an instant read thermometer registers 125F. Remove from the oven and rest for 10 minutes before serving.

Nutritional Info: Calories: 438, Sodium: 100 mg, Dietary Fiber: 1.9 g, Fat: 22.5 g, Carbs: 3.8 g, Protein: 51.1 g.

Sun Dried Tomato Pasta

Using your Nesco SnackMaster to make sun-dried tomatoes is a great way to ensure robust flavors. Fresh basil and garlic add complexity and a bright finish.

Prep time: 10 minutes | Cook time: 15 minutes | Servings: 4

Ingredients:

1 lb. penne pasta

1 cup dehydrated tomatoes

1/4 cup olive oil

1 cup fresh basil

4 cloves garlic, chopped

1/4 cup Parmesan cheese, grated

Instructions:

1. in a food processor, combine the tomatoes, oil, basil, garlic, and half of the Parmesan cheese. Pulse until well combined but not smooth.

2. Boil a pot of water and cook the penne until al dente and drain.

3. In a large bowl, combine the pasta and tomato mixture. Stir well and top with remaining Parmesan cheese to serve.

Nutritional Info: Calories: 498, Sodium: 378 mg, Dietary Fiber: 1.8 g, Fat: 17.2 g, Carbs: 71 g, Protein: 17.4 g.

Vegetarian Lasagna

Lasagna seems like a dish that takes a long time to prepare, but if you use your Nesco SnackMaster to prepare vegetables ahead of time, you can have a delicious lasagna ready in no time.

Prep time: 15 minutes | Cook time: 45 minutes | Servings: 8

Ingredients:

1 box lasagna noodles

12 oz. ricotta cheese

12 oz. mozzarella cheese

1/2 cup Parmesan cheese

1 large eggplant, sliced into rounds and dehydrated

2 zucchini, sliced into rounds and dehydrated

2 yellow squash, sliced into rounds and dehydrated

1/2 lb. spinach, chopped

1 28 oz. can San Marzano Tomatoes, crushed

2 cloves garlic, minced

1 cup fresh basil, chopped

1 tablespoon fresh thyme

2 tablespoons olive oil

Instructions:

1. In a large bowl, combine the cheeses and stir well.

2. In a saucepan, combine tomatoes, garlic, basil, and olive oil over medium heat. Simmer for 10 minutes and remove from heat.

3. Place a small amount of tomato sauce in the bottom of a baking dish. Layer eggplant, pasta, zucchini, yellow squash, & spinach.

4. Add a layer of cheese and sauce to each layer of vegetables.

5. Continue layering until you run out of vegetables or that pan is full. Make sure the top layer is cheese mixture. Cover with foil and bake for 30 minutes. Remove the foil and bake an additional 15 minutes.

Nutritional Info: Calories: 333, Sodium: 409 mg, Dietary Fiber: 6.1 g, Fat: 16.7 g, Carbs: 25.6 g, Protein: 24.7 g.

Trout with Herbs and Citrus

Fresh trout filets have a delicate but unique flavor. The combination of freshly dehydrated citrus and herbs add just the right amount of acid and flavor.

Prep time: 15 minutes | Cook time: 15 minutes | Servings: 2

Ingredients:

2 trout filets.

1 lemon, sliced and dehydrated

1 teaspoon garlic, minced

1 tablespoon parsley, dehydrated

1 tablespoon oregano, dehydrated

2 tablespoons olive oil

Salt and black pepper

Instructions:

1. Brush the trout with olive oil and season with salt and pepper. In the cavity of each trout place two lemon slices and half of the garlic and oregano. Place another two lemon slices on top of each trout and sprinkle with parsley.

2. Heat your oven to 375F. and place the trout in a baking dish. Place the trout in the oven for 10 to 15 minutes or until an instant read thermometer reads 150F.

Nutritional Info: Calories: 400, Sodium: 432 mg, Dietary Fiber: 26 g, Fat: 26.2 g, Carbs: 26 g, Protein: 20.4 g.

Mushroom Risotto

This classic risotto dish is made even easier and full of earthy flavors using mushrooms you've dehydrated using your Nesco SnackMaster.

Prep time: 5 minutes | Cook time: 30 minutes | Servings: 4

Ingredients:

1 cup Arborio rice

3 tablespoons butter

1 cup cremini mushrooms, sliced and dehydrated

3 cups chicken stock

1/2 cup dry white wine

1 tablespoon shallot

1 teaspoon garlic, minced

1/2 teaspoon black pepper

1/4 cup Parmesan cheese, grated

Instructions:

1. In a medium pot, heat the butter until melted. Add the shallot and cook until translucent. Add the rice and stir until all of the grains are coated. Add the wine and simmer until mostly reduced.

2. Add the mushrooms and begin adding chicken stock 1/2 cup at a time. Stir frequently, and when the stock is nearly reduced, add another half cup. When rice is al dente, remove from heat and stir in pepper and Parmesan cheese.

Nutritional Info: Calories: 310, Sodium: 705 mg, Dietary Fiber: 1.5 g, Fat: 10.8 g, Carbs: 41 g, Protein: 6.6 g.

Chili Rubbed Pork Loin

This spicy take on a traditional pork loin is sure to be a hit, and you can use chilies you've dehydrated in your Nesco SnackMaster for an extra kick of heat.

Prep time: 15 minutes | Cook time: 35 minutes | Servings: 2

Ingredients:

1 lb. pork loin

3 red chili peppers, dehydrated

1 tablespoon garlic, minced

Salt and black pepper

2 tablespoons vegetable oil

Instructions:

1. Season the pork loin with salt and pepper. Heat the oil in a large skillet over high heat until smoking. Add the pork loin and turn to brown on all sides.

2. Remove the pork from the pan and place on a cutting board.

3. Place the chili peppers in a food processor and pulse until a fine powder form.

4. Rub the pork loin with garlic and then with chili powder. Place in a baking dish and place in oven for 30 minutes. Remove from oven and allow to rest for 10 minutes before slicing.

Nutritional Info: Calories: 644, Sodium: 170 mg, Dietary Fiber: 0.3 g, Fat: 43.2 g, Carbs: 2.4 g, Protein: 58.5 g.

13

SIDES

Pickle Chips

Pickles are a classic snack or side dish, but they don't exactly travel well. What if you could take pickles on the go without the mess. Thanks to your Nesco SnackMaster, you can!

Prep time: 5 minutes | Cook time: 12 hours | Servings: 12

Ingredients:

1 jar large dill pickles

Instructions:

1. Remove pickles from the jar and pat dry with paper towels. Slice the pickles length-wise into long, thin slabs about 1/4 inch thick.

2. Lay the pickle slices on the racks of your Nesco SnackMaster and set to 125F. Dehydrate for 12 hours or until the pickles are completely dried.

3. Remove from the racks and eat like chips or store and rehydrate when needed. To rehydrate simply place the dried pickle slices in a bowl of lukewarm water and wait 5 to 10 minutes.

Nutritional Info: Calories: 1, Sodium: 98 mg, Dietary Fiber: 0.1 g, Fat: 0 g, Carbs: 0.3 g, Protein: 0.1 g.

Beet Chips

Beets are a great source of valuable nutrients and these beet chips are the perfect way to keep delicious beets fresh for whenever you want to enjoy them.

Prep time: 12 hours | Cook time: 12 hours | Servings: 10

Ingredients:

4 large beets sliced into thin rounds

1 cup apple cider vinegar

Instructions:

1. In a wide shallow bowl or tray, pour the vinegar and arrange the beet slices in a single layer. Allow the beet slices to soak for 12 hours.

2. Remove the beets from the vinegar and pat dry with paper towels.

3. Lay the beet slices on the racks of your Nesco SnackMaster and set to 125F. Dehydrate for 12 hours or until beet slices are completely dried. Store in zip-lock bags until ready to use.

Nutritional Info: Calories: 23, Sodium: 32 mg, Dietary Fiber: 0.8 g, Fat: 0.1 g, Carbs: 4.2 g, Protein: 0.7 g.

Classic Stuffing

This holiday staple is easy to make and goes with a wide variety of different dishes. Your Nesco SnackMaster lets you prepare the ingredients ahead so your stuffing can be made at a moment's notice.

Prep time: 15 minutes | Cook time: 6 hours | Servings: 4

Ingredients:

2 cups white bread cubed

3 tablespoons parsley, chopped

1 teaspoon chicken stock powder (see recipe: 65)

1 tablespoon onion, minced

3 tablespoons celery, minced

1 teaspoon fresh thyme

1/2 teaspoon black pepper

1/2 teaspoon salt

Instructions:

1. In a large bowl, combine the bread, parsley, chick stock powder, onion, celery, thyme, salt and pepper. Stir well to combine.

2. Place the mixture in even layers in your Nesco SnackMaster and set to 125F. Dehydrate for 6 hours. Store stuffing in a large zip-lock bag.

3. To rehydrate stuffing when ready to use, place contents of the bag in a large pot and add 1/2 cup water and 1/4 cup melted butter over low heat. Stir until stuffing is warm and serve.

Nutritional Info: Calories: 52, Sodium: 509 mg, Dietary Fiber: 0.8 g, Fat: 0.7 g, Carbs: 9.9 g, Protein: 1.6 g.

Zesty Salsa

This flavorful salsa is perfect for any occasion and because your Nesco SnackMaster allows you to preserve the ingredients, you can make up a fresh batch whenever you want.

Prep time: 20 minutes | Cook time: 6 hours | Servings: 12

Ingredients:

---

1 yellow onion, chopped

4 Jalapeño peppers, chopped and most seeds removed

4 cloves garlic, minced

1/4 cup orange juice

Juice of 4 limes

1 cup tomatoes, chopped

1 teaspoon salt

1/2 teaspoon black pepper

1/4 cup cilantro leaves

Instructions:

---

1. Chop all vegetables and place in a large bowl. Add the orange and lime juice and stir well to combine. Season with salt and pepper.

2. Place Clean-A-Screens on the racks of your SnackMaster and set to 115F. Dehydrate for 6 hours.

3. To rehydrate, place desired amount of salsa in a bowl and gradually add cold water until you reach the consistency you prefer.

Nutritional Info: Calories: 15, Sodium: 318 mg, Dietary Fiber: 0.7 g, Fat: 0.1 g, Carbs: 4 g, Protein: 0.5 g.

Pomodoro Sauce

This classic Italian sauce is easy to make and thanks to your Nesco SnackMaster, you can make a large batch and then rehydrate however much you need.

Prep time: 30 minutes | Cook time: 12 hours | Servings: 6

Ingredients:

2 28 oz. cans whole tomatoes

1 yellow onion, chopped

4 cloves garlic, minced

1/4 cup basil

1/4 cup green pepper, chopped

1 sprig thyme

Instructions:

1. Place the tomatoes in a food processor and pulse until chunky but not smooth. Add the onion, garlic, green pepper, basil, and thyme. Pulse several times to combine.

2. Place Clean-A-Screens on the racks of your Nesco SnackMaster and spread the tomato sauce evenly on the screens. Set your SnackMaster to 135F and dehydrate for 12 hours. Store sauce in zip-lock bags until ready to use.

3. To rehydrate sauce, place 1 cup of dehydrated sauce powder with 1/2 cup boiling water and stir until warm.

Nutritional Info: Calories: 61, Sodium: 15 mg, Dietary Fiber: 4 g, Fat: 0.6 g, Carbs: 13.3 g, Protein: 2.8 g.

Black Beans and Rice

This simple yet filling dish is perfect for dinner after a busy day, or as a hearty side dish on a camping or hiking trip.

Prep time: 20 minutes | Cook time: 6 hours | Servings: 4

Ingredients:

1 cup white rice, cooked

1/2 cup chicken breast, cubed

1/2 cup black beans, steamed

1/4 cup green bell pepper, chopped

2 tablespoons cilantro

1/2 teaspoon garlic powder

1 tablespoon vegetable oil

Instructions:

1. In a small skillet, heat oil over medium heat and add the chicken. Cook until cooked through and remove from heat.

2. In a large bowl, combine the chicken, rice, beans, bell pepper, cilantro, and garlic powder. Mix well.

3. Place Clean-A-Screens on the racks of your Nesco SnackMaster and spread the mixture evenly on the screens. Set your SnackMaster to 125F and dehydrate for 6 hours. Store mixture in zip-lock bags until ready to use.

4. To rehydrate, combine the contents of the bag with 1 1/4 cup boiling water and stir well. Cover and let stand 10 minutes before serving.

Nutritional Info: Calories: 317, Sodium: 18 mg, Dietary Fiber: 4.4 g, Fat: 4.8 g, Carbs: 52.9 g, Protein: 14.6 g.

Spicy Corn Salsa

This salsa has a definite kick of heat, but it also incorporates sweet corn and rich beans for a perfectly balance flavor and texture.

Prep time: 10 minutes | Cook time: 6 hours | Servings: 12

Ingredients:

2 cans yellow corn

2 cans black beans

1 tomato, chopped

1/2 cup cilantro, chopped

1/2 red onion, finely chopped

1 red bell pepper, chopped

1 clove garlic, minced

Juice from 2 limes

2 Jalapeño peppers, finely chopped

1 tablespoon olive oil

Instructions:

1. In a large bowl, combine all ingredients. Stir well to combine.

2. Place Clean-A-Screens on the racks of your Nesco SnackMaster and spread the salsa evenly on the screens. Set your SnackMaster to 135F and dehydrate for 6 hours or until everything is completely dried. Store in zip-lock bags.

3. To rehydrate salsa, pour in a small amount of cold water and stir until desired consistency is reached.

Nutritional Info: Calories: 170, Sodium: 212 mg, Dietary Fiber: 6.3 g, Fat: 2.2 g, Carbs: 31.8 g, Protein: 8.6 g.

Lemon Cookies

Cornbread adds such a fantastic dimension to traditional stuffing because of its sweet flavors and complex texture. This stuffing is sure to be a hit with friends and family.

Prep time: 20 minutes | Cook time: 6 hours | Servings: 6

Ingredients:

1 lb. corn bread, cubed

6 slices white bread, cubed

12 saltine crackers, crushed

1 cup butter, melted

3 stalks celery, chopped

1/2 onion chopped

6 cups chicken stock

6 eggs, beaten

1/2 cup buttermilk

Instructions:

1. Combine all ingredients in a large bowl and stir well. Place in a baking dish.

2. Heat oven to 350F and bake stuffing for 10 minutes. Remove from oven and allow to cool.

3. Place Clean-A-Screens on the racks of your SnackMaster and spread the stuffing evenly over the racks. Set the dehydrator to 135F and dehydrate for 6 hours. When completely dried, remove from the racks and store in a zip-lock bag.

4. To rehydrate stuffing, drizzle in warm water until moist.

Nutritional Info: Calories: 668, Sodium: 845 mg, Dietary Fiber: 1.2 g, Fat: 43.8 g, Carbs: 54.8 g, Protein: 15 g.

Tomato Cream Sauce

This simple and delicious sauce is perfect for poultry or pasta. Simply add a bit of milk and your dehydrated sauce will spring to life whenever you need it.

Prep time: 15 minutes | Cook time: 8 hours | Servings: 6

Ingredients:

1 cup tomatoes, dehydrated

1 cup heavy cream

1/4 cup yellow onion, finely chopped

2 cloves garlic, minced

1/2 cup chicken broth

2 tablespoon vegetable oil

1/2 teaspoon black pepper

Instructions:

1. In a medium saucepan heat oil over medium heat. Add the onion and cook until translucent. Add the garlic and cook and additional two minutes. Add the tomatoes and cook several minutes. Add the chicken broth and pepper and simmer until tomatoes have broken down. Add the cream and simmer an additional five minutes before removing from heat.

2. Place Clean-A-Screens on the racks of your SnackMaster and spread a thin layer of the sauce onto each screen. Set your dehydrator to 135F and dehydrate for 8 hours.

3. Remove dried sauce from the racks and store in zip-lock bags until ready to use.

4. To rehydrate sauce, mix with 1/4 cup warm water and stir.

Nutritional Info: Calories: 122, Sodium: 73 mg, Dietary Fiber: 0.5 g, Fat: 12.1 g, Carbs: 2.7 g, Protein: 1.2 g.

Potato Chips

The classic potato chip is simple, crispy and delicious. They also usually require frying in oil which is messy and time consuming. These easy chips are light crispy and require no frying at all.

Prep time: 10 minutes | Cook time: 6 hours | Servings: 6

Ingredients:

2 russet potatoes, peeled   salt

vegetable oil spray

Instructions:

1. Rinse and peel the potatoes and use a mandolin to slice them into thin rounds. Lay the rounds on a baking sheet and spray with cooking oil on both side.

2. Sprinkle the rounds with salt and place on the racks of your SnackMaster. Set to 110F and dehydrate for 6 hours or until the chips are dried and crispy.

3. Store in a large zip-lock bag until ready to use.

Nutritional Info: Calories: 49, Sodium: 4 mg, Dietary Fiber: 1.7 g, Fat: 0.1 g, Carbs: 11.2 g, Protein: 1.2 g.

14

DESSERTS

Cranberry Scones

These easy to make scones are delicious, tender, and surprisingly healthy. Serve them for breakfast or a refreshing dessert.

Prep time: 30 minutes | Cook time: 6 hours | Servings: 12

Ingredients:

4 apples, grated

1 cup fresh cranberries

2 tablespoons honey

2 cups almonds, ground

2 cups carrots, grated

1 cup flax seed

1 cup water

3 tablespoons coconut oil, melted

Instructions:

1. In a large bowl, combine all ingredients.

2. Place Clean-A-Screens on the racks of your Nesco SnackMaster.

3. Use a large spoon to place balls of the dough onto the screens and set your SnackMaster to 115F. Dehydrate for 3 hours, flip the scones, and then continue dehydrating an additional 3 hours.

Nutritional Info: Calories: 232, Sodium: 17 mg, Dietary Fiber: 7.1 g, Fat: 14.4 g, Carbs: 21.8 g, Protein: 5.4 g.

Cinnamon Apple Cookies

Looking for a healthy alternative to traditional cookies? Look no further than these amazingly flavorful apple cookies made directly in your Nesco SnackMaster.

Prep time: 40 minutes | Cook time: 12 hours | Servings: 6

Ingredients:

4 apples, chopped

2 teaspoons ground cinnamon

1 teaspoon nutmeg

2 teaspoons vanilla

1/2 teaspoon salt

3 bananas

1 cup dates

Instructions:

1. Place the apples and bananas in a food processor and pulse until almost smooth. Add the cinnamon, nutmeg, vanilla, salt, and dates. Pulse until nearly smooth.

2. Place Clean-A-Screens on the racks of your Nesco SnackMaster.

3. Spoon balls of the dough onto the screens and flatten with the back of a spoon. Set your SnackMaster to 115F and dehydrate for 12 hours.

Nutritional Info: Calories: 221, Sodium: 197 mg, Dietary Fiber: 8 g, Fat: 0.7 g, Carbs: 57.3 g, Protein: 1.8 g.

Carrot Cake

These fun carrot cupcakes are easy to make and healthier than regular carrot cake. Best of all, your Nesco SnackMaster ensures perfect flavor and texture.

Prep time: 30 minutes | Cook time: 9 hours | Servings: 6

Ingredients:

3 cups carrots, grated

1 teaspoon cinnamon

1/2 teaspoon nutmeg

1/4 teaspoon ground cloves

1 cup pecans, crushed

1/2 cup shredded coconut

1/4 cup water

1/2 teaspoon salt

Instructions:

1. In a food processor, combine the pecans and coconut and pulse.

2. In a large bowl, combine the carrots, pecans, coconut, cinnamon, nutmeg, cloves, water, and salt.

3. Place Clean-A-Screens on the racks of your Nesco SnackMaster.

4. Form the dough into individual cakes about 4 inches across. Place the cakes onto the screens and set your SnackMaster to 165F.

5. Dehydrate for one hour, then lower the temperature to 125F and dehydrate for another 8 hours.

Nutritional Info: Calories: 211, Sodium: 234 mg, Dietary Fiber: 4.7 g, Fat: 19 g, Carbs: 10.2 g, Protein: 3.2 g.

Lemon Cookies

These lightly sweetened cookies are a perfect snack or light dessert for those looking to cut down on sugar while still enjoying satisfying treat.

Prep time: 20 minutes | Cook time: 8 hours | Servings: 15

Ingredients:

Juice from 2 lemons

2 cups cashews

1 banana

1/2 cups honey

2 cups shredded coconut

1 teaspoon vanilla

Instructions:

1. In a food processor, combine the lemon juice, cashews, banana, honey, coconut, and vanilla. Pulse until smooth.

2. Use a spoon to place dough onto the racks of your SnackMaster and use the back of the spoon to flatten them. Set your SnackMaster to 115F and dehydrate for 8 hours.

Nutritional Info: Calories: 187, Sodium: 6 mg, Dietary Fiber: 1.8 g, Fat: 12.1 g, Carbs: 19.3 g, Protein: 3.3 g.

Peach Cobbler

Yes, you read that right. You can make authentic peach cobbler in your Nesco SnackMaster. It's perfect for camping or picnics.

Prep time: 10 minutes | Cook time: 8 hours | Servings: 4

Ingredients:

2 peaches sliced into 1/4-inch slices

1/3 cup bread crumbs

1 tablespoon sugar

1/2 teaspoon cinnamon

1/2 teaspoon nutmeg

1/2 cup water

Instructions:

1. Place the peach slices on the rack of your SnackMaster and set to 125F. Dehydrate for 8 hours.

2. Remove peach slices from the racks and combine with the breadcrumbs, sugar, cinnamon, and nutmeg. Store in a zip-lock bag until ready to use.

3. To rehydrate, simply combine the contents of the bag with 1/2 cup boiling water and stir.

Nutritional Info: Calories: 78, Sodium: 67 mg, Dietary Fiber: 1.8 g, Fat: 0.8 g, Carbs: 16.9 g, Protein: 1.9 g.

Banana Bread Pudding

This delightful combination of banana bread and bread pudding makes for an easy dessert after a busy day, or on the trails after a long hike.

Prep time: 10 minutes | Cook time: 8 hours | Servings: 4

Ingredients:

2 bananas, sliced into rounds

1/4 cup cashews, chopped

1/2 cup white bread, cut into large chunks

1 tablespoon brown sugar

Instructions:

1. Place the banana slices on the racks of your Nesco SnackMaster and set to 125F. Dehydrate for 8 hours or until completely dried.

2. In a zip-lock bag, combine the bananas and brown sugar. In another zip-lock bag combine the bread chunks and cashews.

3. To rehydrate, combine all ingredients with 1/2 cup warm water and allow to sit for 5 minutes before stirring and serving.

Nutritional Info: Calories: 122, Sodium: 32 mg, Dietary Fiber: 1.9 g, Fat: 4.3 g, Carbs: 20.7 g, Protein: 2.3 g.

Pumpkin Pie Toffee

This easy to make treat is perfect for day trips in the fall. Your Nesco SnackMaster guarantees perfectly even and reliable results.

Prep time: 10 minutes | Cook time: 8 hours | Servings: 4

Ingredients:

1 can pumpkin

1/4 cup maple syrup

1/2 teaspoon cinnamon

1/2 teaspoon nutmeg

1/2 teaspoon ground ginger

1/2 teaspoon allspice

Instructions:

1. In a large bowl, combine the pumpkin, spices, and maple syrup and mix well.

2. Place Clean-A-Screens on the racks of your SnackMaster and spread the pumpkin mixture about 1/8 inch thick.

3. Set your SnackMaster to 135F and dehydrate for 8 hours.

Nutritional Info: Calories: 76, Sodium: 5 mg, Dietary Fiber: 2.1 g, Fat: 0.3 g, Carbs: 18.9 g, Protein: 0.7 g.

Apple Cake

This delicious apple cake is easily made ahead of time and can be reheated whenever. Perfect for an easy dessert for the kids, or take it camping for a dessert you don't have to bake.

Prep time: 35 minutes | Cook time: 12 hours | Servings: 6

Ingredients:

2 1/2 cups flour

2 teaspoons baking powder

1 teaspoon baking soda

1/2 teaspoon salt

1 1/2 cups sugar

1 cup applesauce

1 teaspoon vanilla

1 cup egg whites

1 cup milk

Instructions:

1. In a large bowl, combine the flour, baking powder, baking soda, and salt.

2. In another bowl, combine the sugar, applesauce, vanilla, milk and eggs. Mix until eggs are beaten.

3. Stir the dry mixture into the wet mixture and pour into a greased baking dish.

4. Set your oven to 350F and bake for 30 to 35 minutes.

5. Remove the cake from the oven and allow to cool. Cut cake into cubes about 2 inches wide. Place them on the racks of your Nesco SnackMaster and set to 135F. Dehydrate for 12 hours. the cake should be crunchy when finished.

6. To rehydrate, sprinkle boiling water onto the cake chunks and allow them to sit for 5 minutes.

Nutritional Info: Calories: 440, Sodium: 468 mg, Dietary Fiber: 1.9 g, Fat: 1.4 g, Carbs: 97.5 g, Protein: 11.2 g.

Berry Crumble

This easy to assemble berry crumble is perfect for all occasions. Your Nesco SnackMaster allows you to make this dish ahead so you can rehydrate whenever you want.

Prep time: 20 minutes | Cook time: 8 hours | Servings: 6

Ingredients:

1 cup oats

3/4 cup flour

1/2 cup brown sugar

3/4 cup white sugar

1/2 teaspoon salt

1 stick butter, cut into pieces

2 cups raspberries

2 cups blueberries

2 cups blackberries

1/2 teaspoon cinnamon

Instructions:

1. Place the berries on the racks of your Nesco SnackMaster and set to 125F. Dehydrate for 8 hours.

2. In a large bowl, combine the oats, 1/2 cup of flour, 1/2 cup white sugar, brown sugar, and salt. Add the butter and stir until butter is fully incorporated. Place the mixture in a baking dish and set your oven to 350F. Bake for 1 hour and remove to cool.

3. When the berries are finished dehydrating, remove from the SnackMaster and place in a zip-lock bag with the remaining flour, sugar, and cinnamon.

4. When ready to rehydrate, add 1/4 cup boiling water to the bag with the berries and stir until rehydrated. Top with crumble topping and serve.

Nutritional Info: Calories: 453, Sodium: 308 mg, Dietary Fiber: 8.3 g, Fat: 17 g, Carbs: 74.7 g, Protein: 5.1 g.

Apple Pie

This all-American classic can be made with the convenience of your Nesco SnackMaster, and brings out the complex delicious flavors of tart green apples.

Prep time: 30 minutes | Cook time: 12 hours | Servings: 4

Ingredients:

2 cups granny smith apple slices

2 cups flour

3 tablespoons butter, cubed

1/2 teaspoon salt

1 teaspoon baking powder

1 egg, beaten

1/2 cup milk

1 teaspoon cinnamon

2 tablespoons sugar

Instructions:

1. Place the apple slices on the racks of your Nesco SnackMaster and set to 135F and dehydrate for 12 hours.

2. In a large bowl, combine the flour, baking powder, salt, butter, milk and egg. Mix until you have a smooth dough. Divide the dough into 4 balls and roll flat.

3. Remove apples from the dehydrator and place several slices of apple into each piece of dough. Fold the dough over and press to seal. You can bake the pies in the oven at 350 for 20 minutes, or deep fry for an even crisper crust.

Nutritional Info: Calories: 400, Sodium: 384 mg, Dietary Fiber: 3 g, Fat: 11 g, Carbs: 65.3 g, Protein: 9 g.

Made in the USA
Las Vegas, NV
29 March 2024

87967037R00092